Walking down Deansgate

By

Tom Molloy

RB
Rossendale Books

Other publications by this author:

*Everything But The Beach: A Slice
Of Manchester Life (2013)*

*Hale to Mumps: More Slices
Of Manchester Life (2014)*

Football Anorak 2014/2015 (2015)

Published by Lulu Enterprises Inc.
3101 Hillsborough Street
Suite 210
Raleigh, NC 27607-5436
United States of America

Published in paperback 2015
Category: Non-Fiction
Copyright Tom Molloy © 2020
ISBN : 978-0-244-55522-1

Dedication

To Ali, Roxy and Kilo

Acknowledgements

With special thanks to Phil Griffin, John Ireland, Wolfgang Buttress, Ruth Estevez and the only 3 people to have read the previous 3 books, Bernard O'Hearns (Shell Racing Club), Ken Jones's daughter and Stuart Brodie's mum.

Last but not least, Norwegian Editor: Voxra Andersen Cover Photo: Jan Chlebik

Altrincham

In the 1980s when Altrincham FC were forever killing giants, the
southern press always referred to them as being from an affluent
part of south Manchester. These articles were obviously written
by people who had never ventured into the Axe and Cleaver. The
real big hitters around here live in Dunham and Bowdon and to a
lesser extent Timpers.

Aldringeham only really came to prominence after King Edward
I's charter of 1290 permitted a market here on a Tuesday. Both
Bowdon (town on a curved hill) and Dunham (hill home) are
mentioned in the Doomsday Book of 1086. Timperley was
recorded as having farmsteads as far back as the 8th century.
Even rough-edged Broadheath can boast its own section of
Watling St. Bowdon has always had an aristocratic edge and a
surfeit of silver spoons.

Even back in the 19th century Bowdon contained 'many
mansions' and in 1872, John Marius Wilson, the Imperial
Gazetteer of England described it thus "It enjoys fine air and
charming environs and is a favourite resort of ruralising parties
from Manchester" A century later a survey found only 15% of its
inhabitants to be working class. The rest were indescribably posh.
Dunham belonged to the Masci family of Normandy, hence
Dunham Massey. In 1173 it was recorded as having a motte and
bailey castle. This was a wooden structure, the ancient equivalent
of a convector heater. The last Masci owner of the castle was
Hamon de Massey. When he died in 1341 it passed to Lord of
Knocking, Roger Le Strange, who let it fall into disrepair. The
land eventually becoming part of the Stamford estate who later
left it to the National Trust. A lot of Roger's descendants are still
believed to reside in nearby Timperley, hence the often-heard
phrase "There are a lot of strange people in Timperley"

By 2010 Altrincham's veneer had cracked completely. It was now
the boarded-up shops on the High Street that brought the
journalists to visit the northern capital of fur coat no knickers.
Since then though the transformation of Alty has been
spectacular. The good times always seemed linked to its various
transport links. In 1754 the imposition of a toll on the Chester Rd
diverted much traffic towards Altrincham's market, and in 1765

the extension of the Bridgewater Canal brought an extra direct route into Manchester. Now it is the Metrolink that has brought a Renaissance.

The place is buzzing again thanks to places like Sugo Pasta Kitchen, Belgian Bar, Pi, Porta and Two Brothers Cafe (no relation to the seven drinkers) I loved the slow roast ox cheek with walnuts at Porta and necked a couple of La Virgen Jamonera beer. Checked the beer's score on ratebeer.com and they gave it 1* What is up with these people? It's beer!

The real gem is the oldest surviving area of town around Albert Place and the Old Market. The new incarnation of the market has won many awards with its great food and enthusiastic hubbub. Altrincham was once dubbed 'Bravest town in England' after a record 161 men from the same street (Chapel St) volunteered for service in WW1. You sometimes need to be a brave man to eat in the Market Hall. These ladies who lunch are prepared to use extreme measures to defend their tables and spare chairs.

Outside in front of the Town Hall (1900 C H Hindle) is the impressive Market Trader statue by Colin Spofforth (2007) I couldn't see them, but the town's original stocks are supposed to be nearby where they kept Winsford fans in the 1980s. The outdoor stalls contain lots of old friends. Trove, Honest Crust Pizza, a high-class butcher and wonderful cake maker. You could spend the whole weekend here.

Unexpected Plaque. On Market St at number 16 is a blue plaque to the artist, Helen Allingham (1848-1926) who spent her childhood in Altrincham. The first woman member of the Royal Watercolour Society. Her country cottage scenes are amazing.

Aging Process

The realisation that you've forgotten your glasses just after passing a poster that seemed to say, "The Curious Case of the Dog in the Nightie". Heading to a gig at YES had wanted to grab something to eat in Oishi Noodles just the other side of Oxford Rd. Optimistically taking a menu I immediately had to admit defeat. The writing was way too small. I told the lovely waitress "It's no good I've forgot my specs" "Don't worry I will read it out to you, which she did very loudly, annunciating each word like she was tutoring Forest Gump's slower brother. Young Japanese people looked on sympathetically. Vaguely disturbing at first but then strangely comforting. These people know how to treat their elders. Have been back many times since but have never ever forgot those specs again and since she recommended it on that first visit have been strangely hooked on that lychee soft drink. Soothing.

As well as eyesight and hearing, memory gets a bit foggy. I was hugely excited to see a gig announced at The Talleyrand, Levenshulme by the legendary Stockholm Monsters. 'Wow are they still going?' An evening treat the bar is only a few hundred metres from where I work. When I got there, I spotted the poster "Tonight Bethlehem Casuals 9pm" More than a few hundred metres away, more like a few thousand miles.

This part of East Levenshulme was once known as Talleyrand after the limping philandering French ex bishop and later Napoleonic statesman Charles-Maurice Talleyrand. Admired and distrusted in equal measure he was originally sent to London in 1791 to avert war. Back in France many considered him a traitor and collaborator and called for his head. Talley fled the capital and holed up in rural Levenshulme charming the local ladies with an exaggerated French accent. To this day Talleyrand is a by word for a feckless, cynical, crafty geezer similar to tory. William Pitt eventually expelled him in 1794 and he went on to get a top job with Napoleon. In later life he returned to his Catholic faith, confessed all his sins and was granted extreme unction.

A wild set by the Casuals, that cellist is some talent. What a homely, welcoming place and the small back room venue has fine acoustics. The bar has some great beers and the lounge is like someone's front room. The old lounge lizard would have appreciated this place but maybe not the feminist toilet seat in the tiny cubicles, closing slowly mid-stream causing mild panic. Talleyrand quote "The reputation of a man is like his shadow. Gigantic when it precedes him and pygmy when it follows"

Seemingly having no such age problems is the legendary Martha Reeves still rocking the soul world at a youthful 77. After a riotous reception to "Dancing in the Street" she put both arms out to the side and did a full body shimmy in celebration. A voice at the front shouted, "Shake that body Martha" and she replied. "At my age honey, if I don't shake it, nobody else is going to"

Tune: "Youth" Daughter

Confusing. Young Chorltonite couple arguing on the tram when you slowly realise you don't know what on earth they are talking about. Him "No definitely want to see the new Star Wars tomorrow" Her "Boring. We've been invited to Alberts Schloss" Him "Standing around drinking cocktails looking at posh people wishing you were them. Now that's boring!" Her "They're not posh they send them clothes back next day" Bizarrely they pronounced schloss as schlow. I know it's wrong because I googled it. One night I had the misfortune to be in schlow on what seemed a restrained night. Then Stevie Wonder's 'Sir Duke' came on and it transformed into a scene they would have cut from One Flew over the Cuckoo's Nest. Dozens of insurance brokers dancing about singing and waving the work credit card around. Bring back The Land O' Cakes.

Decorators in Alderley Edge

At one time Alderley Edge was a place of myths and legends. From King Arthur to Posh Spice. Then along came Really Desperate Housewives of Cheshire and things began to slide. Not long after that Wayne Rooney was sacked from his job as designated driver and the cracks in the image became chasms. Today in Yara, the only celeb is a young director celebrating her birthday with mum and dad. Home from a filming trip in Cornwall she was now interested in the new Castaway series. Dad looked far more interested in another bottle of Beirut.

Can only assume the chef was on a break in Lebanon or maybe had gone over the Edge. The food was great on taste and nutrition but would have been slaughtered on MasterChef for presentation. The bourak was fine but the makloubeh resembled something that Frankie Dettori might carry back into the weighing room. Is this what they mean by a saddle of lamb? Think Makloubeh means upside down, maybe I was meant to flip it. Still it was pretty tasty and went down well with a couple of Beiruts. A possible clue was given by the fact front of house was also the barman and "Service please" and "Yes chef" sounded suspiciously like the same voice. Cheapo weekday lunch deal.

Bubble Room with its classy sunny terrace is one of the best people watching spots in the North. So many charlatans up here, most of them using that cashpoint down the side of the Midland.

So dark, no one behind can see that 'No funds available' message flash up

I went straight on the potent and outrageously good Irish Whiskey Smash. The two barmen fought for the chance to make them just to relieve the boredom. The only other bar flies were two old boys drinking and singing the praises of Boddingtons. They had that painter and decorator to the rich look. After an hour or so one of the lads behind the bar tried to wean them onto a real ale infused with blackcurrant. No chance "That's not beer" Then his mate tried them with tasters of Sierra Nevada IPA. Hated it. These were the fussiest guinea pigs on earth. The right vintage but doubt they were ever lucky enough to have tasted the real Cream of Manchester in The Ducie, Strangeways, pumped through golden pipes under the road from brewery to pub to liver. Heavenly. Spoke to one of the decorators on the way back from the latrines and asked him if anywhere else was any good round here. "Not really" This was obviously the place. He struggled, scrunched up his face and asked tentatively "Have you been in The Bigamist?" Might be a local in joke or even a tip but pretty sure he meant Botanist.

Thankfully had the chance to return to Yara a year or so later for a family birthday meal and the food and ambience were top class. The chef indeed must have been captured by a Cheshire Housewife on that previous afternoon. Couldn't resist heading to Bubble for a whiskey nightcap. No decorators tonight, it had more of a window cleaner to the famous vibe, and the biggest percentage of Stella drinkers I've ever noticed in any bar. Man, woman, dog they were all on it and on a Monday night. The staff were excitedly discussing a night out "Millie are you coming to see DJ CK with us?" Had to Google that was a real artist. With a name like that he couldn't go wrong in Alderley Edge.

Aldous and Ethel

If anyone has ever conquered the skill of making each song sound like it's the first time, she has ever sung it, it's Aldous Harding. Then there is the coaxing a tune out of that reluctant guitar. No wonder she is prone to a grimace as she expresses her chasm deep lyrics. She dismisses the depth by saying, the significance escapes even her. What would Kirkie from Corrie do let loose with these words?

"I get so anxious I need a tattoo, something binding that hides me" "Show the ferret to the egg, I'm not getting led along" and in tribute to her native NZ and her new Welsh home "All love is fleece that leaves a cold lamb laughing in the breeze"

If you turned for a moment from the stage to look at one of the many nutters here tonight, you'd be excused for thinking another vocalist had stepped forward. Such is the range and variation of her voice.

Complete silence while she played but then a strange bedlam as she re-tuned. You sometimes wonder if those train fumes do leak in from the tracks above Gorilla. The mad hecklers, the woman with hiccups drinking out of the wrong side of a can of Red Stripe. The stranger next to her asking "Do you want a Nicorette?"

My nemesis was a big old lump from Middlesbrough "We drove down this morning and have been on it all day" He kept stumbling back into me giving a mouthful of overgrown Teesside ponytail, drunken apology and resume swaying. Nowhere to hide for any of us in that area, we all got a taste of Timotei during the gig.

Aldous (real name Hannah) tuning away between songs "My mind is saying tell them a funny story while you tune" Then in a deeper voice of warning "But remember what happened the last time you tried that" "Anyway my psychiatrist told me. Only do one thing at a time" Another big bruiser near the back bar who had his girlfriend in a kind of judo hold blurted out in a thick Oldham accent "Try telling that t' my girlfriend" Strangely she looked very proud.

AH does seem to have some artistic freedom. Her set list is said to differ each night. Mistakenly she asked for requests and the natives each side of the stage became even more restless. She suggested they write their chosen song on their forehead and then fought it out to decide the winner. A dangerous dare at some gigs! Still pondering whether to play an old or new song a voice in the middle shouted "Why not a Blend?" (Blend is an old AH song)

He then stood there with a Piers Morgan smug smirk waiting for a round of applause. From the second row came a voice trying to calm things "We are all having a great time" but he sounded like John Barrowman after a few wines. Aldous glanced over, eyebrows raised "He gets really violent later"

Special mention to lovely Aussie support act Laura Jean "I love Manchester. I'm not even lying" Laura had made the cardinal error of reading the comments made after her review in The Guardian. The one that said she 'lacked charisma and a sense of humour' had stood on her karma. Best to remember it could have been written by someone like Smoggie, Nicorette, Oldhamite, Piers, Barrowman or worse.

Aldous had returned the favour of Laura's musical support with a deadpan first line of "I'm charismatic and funny as well" At the encore another mouthful of pony tail for me but this time there was enough space to push him away, he didn't go far as he had the balance of a Subbuteo player. He lurched forward and made a drunken apology and like the Alaskan cop confronted by a Grizzly "I could smell his breath and see the fish on his teeth" Way too close.

As the lights went up, karma did make an appearance. He tried to roll his empty can to the wall like a bowler at next-door All-Star Lanes and satisfyingly he followed right after it. Think he was going to curdle my opinion of the night so was lucky to see Bonnie from the Peveril in Gorilla's bar. "What did you make of that?" Almost speechless "I just love her"

Future problems for Aldous. Her next Manchester gig is due to be at Academy 2. Can she produce such an intense performance in a place that could suck the soul out of a Gospel choir?

Top Tune: Aldous Harding "The Barrel"

Hadn't really heard much about Methyl Ethel just the fact that they were from the cultural hotbed of Perth, Western Australia. Even people from Perth consider it an artistic desert. It's almost a carnival atmosphere in YES's Pink Room tonight and there are plenty of jovial Aussies. It always amazes me the fan base bands have. If an Eskimo band played a midweek gig in Manchester, they would somehow bring a huge following in furry parkas. Everyone seems really chatty tonight including a lad at the bar who says, "Why do they call this the Pink Room?" "Think it's an undercoat" He is from Bristol and runs a countrywide legal recruitment firm. A lover of music and indie expert when in another city he always goes to a live gig. He told me that I wouldn't believe the number of great musicians in his industry and that he is actually in a group with other legal types, that play at corporate events, Band of Lawyers? That's a gig I need to see. I told him I worked in a huge factory and nobody can even play a tambourine.

After spotting that the woman next to me at the bar had a Claddagh ring on, I tried to pass on the friendly vibe "Ah a Claddagh ring. Are you from Galway?" "No! It was a gift" and looked at me like I'd asked if she was in the Gestapo. At the mixing desk the atmosphere had also changed. Ethel had brought along their own mixing man leaving the two locals twiddling their thumbs. A lad approached the desk saying the sound at the front was awful and they basically gagged him, leaving the Aussie mixer in ignorant bliss. Really enjoyable night, met a buzzing fellow gig goer on the hike up the stairs from base camp to Oxford Rd station and my Ethel knowledge was blown to bits "You into their stuff?" "Yeah, especially the last album" I guessed "No way. The second album man, it rocks"

Top Tune: Methyl Ethel "Ubu"

Alternative Manc Top 30

(1) Keith "Back there"
(2) Railway Children "Brighter"
(3) Chameleons "Up the down escalator"
(4) Easterhouse "Out on your own"
(5) 52nd Street "Tell me"
(6) Bodines "Heard it all"
(7) Yargo "Help"
(8) Durutti Column "Sketch for summer"
(9) Waltones "She looks right through me"
(10) World of Twist "The storm"
(11) Puressence "It doesn't matter anymore"
(12) Kalima "Smiling hour"

(13) The High "Up and down"
(14) Dislocation Dance "You'll never know"
(15) Man from Delmonte "My love is like a gift you can't return"
(16) I am Kloot "Same deep water as me"
(17) Big Flame "Why pop stars can't dance"
(18) Ruthless Rap Assassin's "And it wasn't a dream"
(19) Intastella "People"
(20) The Distractions "Time goes by so slow"
(21) Paris Angels "Perfume"
(22) Northside "My rising star"
(23) New Fast Automatic Daffodils" Big"
(24) Doves "Black and white town"
(25) Northern Uproar "From a window"
(26) Stockholm Monsters "Life's two faces"
(27) Marcel King "Reach for love"
(28) The Dooleys "Love of my life"
(29) St Winifred's School Choir "There's no one quite like grandma"
(30) Oasis "Supersonic"
Disq: Barclay James Harvest, Van der Graaf Generator

Ancoats

Despite the endorsement of being Travel Supermarkets 'Number 1 UK Hip Hang Out Neighbourhood' and ranked third coolest in Europe, this 'vibrant community' can be more difficult to find than a Remain voter in Darlington. Plenty of Japanese tourists searching for this cultural nirvana but even they keep the lens caps on.

The old mills are fantastic to look at and the streets and canals reek of history but at the moment it's still more building site than Haight-Ashbury.

For me unlike marauding Sheffield United fans, I found it hard to locate Cutting Room Square. Ask a street sweeper, especially a heavily tattooed one, they always know. "Never heard of it mate. There's a bit of green down there, that might be it" and pointed back across Great Ancoats Street. An Asian woman hurtling passed in a very tight leopard print skirt 'Scuse me are you local?'

No was her answer to everything. Luckily salvation came from a tall blonde "Ha! This is Cutting Room Square. There's not much here is there. Well, there's Rudy's (the 'world famous 'pizzeria that has been crowbarred into a corner of the square under a car park) Oh but that's closed on Mondays. Seven Brothers is definitely open. It's my dad's bar" Civilisation refound.

Ancoats certainly has history, having played a crucial part in the Industrial Revolution. It fell into horrendous decline but was then partially Urban Splashed in the 1980's. First mentioned as Elnecot in 1212, it had grown to eight hamlets a century later and now known as Ana Cots "the lonely cottages"

The transport conduit of the Rochdale Canal in the 1760's brought work and a huge increase in population mainly of Irish and Italian immigrants. By 1790 there were numerous new mills and other workplaces. Sixty years later the population of Ancoats had grown so large it now exceeded that of large Lancastrian mill towns like Blackburn. Cotton and glass industries flourished up until the 1930's when the largest employer became printing, based in Owen Williams palatial glass Daily Express building. Cultural Highlights. The Halle Orchestra use the local St Peter's church for practice and occasional concerts. LS Lowry's 'Ancoats Hospital Outpatients' hangs in The Whitworth Gallery. The legendary Sankey's club nights were held in the former Beehive Mill and Morrissey credited the backing vocals on 'Big Mouth Strikes Again' to Anna Coates.

Lowlights. Larger than his suit, alternative to comedy Bernard Manning was born in Ancoats. Complete with smug look, fag, pint and radical view on immigration, a sort of prototype Farage. Bernard was so working class even his club was named after a packet of fags.

Now I had my bearings a bit of sustenance was needed before an afternoon in Seven Brothers. I headed back up to the very fine Water Side Cafe up by the Rochdale Canal. A lovely breakfast but I'm sure the portion size was directed more at some of the body beautifuls jogging passed and not a trainee darts pro. Still hungry I had to order a meatball sandwich to go. While waiting and enjoying the tunes I asked the proprietor "Where's this music from?" "Syria" and his moustache visibly sagged as he said it. Very sad and a conversation closer.

Seven Brothers have a fantastic stripped back, brick and wood space. Joyously it is in the old Ice Plant building that used to provide the most exciting word of our childhood, Granellis. Part of the Genoan ice cream making family had settled in Ancoats and made summer days perfect.

I settled near the bar and quality tested, The Session (3.8%) Watermelon Wheat (4.5%) IPA (5%)

English IPA (can't remember) and some red stuff I can barely recall. All excellent. At one time a concerned sheepish patron approached the barman J "Did I leave my bag in here Friday night?" "Berghaus? Yes, we have it" Sign of a great bar and beer. He had probably been on the red stuff.

Some of the Seven Brothers arrived (there are four sisters as well. A moderate sized Irish family). Fantastically they were there to meet a Japanese buyer who arrived with his Baltimore sidekick. Their mission to source Real Ale in a can not a bottle. The beer was the real thing, but I wasn't sure about these two. Peter Sellers talking to Cato sounded more authentic. Anyway, they had a great tasting sesh then hurried off to Track Brewery for another appointment. Hugely entertaining.

Couldn't leave the area without a visit to an old friend just around the corner, The Shamrock (1808). It has one of the most sensational reviews on Trip Advisor "Only called in for directions, and one of the pub's four dogs bit me" It's always seemed friendly to me. August Bank Holiday in Ireland, Mayo are trouncing Roscommon on the telly and the Guinness is perfect. Sadly, the dear old Shamrock and a slice of Manchester history passed away just months later. Landlord Gerry said they couldn't hold off the developers any longer. Locals were being pushed aside by gentrification. Truly a crying shame. Think I preferred Ancoats as eight lonely hamlets.

Manc Albums (a)

(1) Howard's boys 'The correct use of soap' 1980
(2) Dance pop 'Elegant swimming' 1993
(3) The first of 31! or is it 32? 'Live at the witch trials' 1979
(4) Dance from the Moss 'Hot lemonade' 1989
(5) Bolton lads 'Thirst for romance' 2007

Art Fair

Manchester Art Fair previously known as Buy Art Fair is always fantastic entertainment. Preview night on the Friday is best. An unseemly scramble to finish the free wine before it goes off. Locusts would baulk at the intensity. An Art Fair virgin might just think that Hockney had arrived with an original, when in fact it's just the wine waiter with more bottles. That's just the punters. The exhibitors can be even more feral and brutal, harshly criticising other people's work and even their neighbour's stalls. As one London artist put it in classic Ab Fab tones "Galleristas are just the worst for bitching"

Away from the competitiveness, those who do get on forge friendships for life, including one married couple who had met here two years ago. The after party poured its way through The Refuge and on to Fab Cafe. The fabulous Nitta, 'a performance artist' from Rotterdam dressed in a leopard print catsuit led the dancing and formed an unholy alliance with a Manchester charity group that stayed on the floor all night long. The next day Nitta re-appeared high fiving everyone and shouting "Wow what a night" just as the charity manager was being introduced to the head of the UK Arts Council.

Sadly, I missed another highlight. A bobble hatted Owen Hargreaves tripping over "Pain in the Arse" a cardboard and papier-mache creation by Robin Broadley, that depicts a half-squeezed pile ointment tube. Luckily no damage to the exhibit and skilfully Owen managed to keep his balance. Ashley Young would probably have been sent sprawling. Robin (one-time Pev barman) is believed to be the greatest living artist from Preston. In fact, the only living artist from Preston.

This year's event took place at Manchester Central just days after the Tories had left but luckily the council had seen fit to fully fumigate the place. My favourite stall holders were the very deep couple from down south. She was very deep in an arty sense and he was very deep into his second bottle of wine. He left a little stash quite near to where they were exhibiting on the outside table of the bar. Naturally this being Manchester when he was not there it was all immediately hoovered up by passing gannets. One girl in a multi coloured Huggy Bear jacket swanned up gracefully and took two full glasses. He was horrified when he returned to the den and left a little note with the next two glasses "Hands off still being drunk" As if that would stop them. He explained to me it was the wife who was the artist and he was merely here to hang the paintings up. On a final lap of the hall I noticed a big crowd around their stall. Great stuff, things are going well. Instead one of the paintings had fallen off the wall. I give you one job!

Desperate Journalist; Bad day at the Office

After a desperately bad one (well office is stretching it) I took a last-minute decision to head to Soup Kitchen to see Desperate Journalist.

These are a fantastic band who seem to go under all radar. Maybe It's simply because most people say "How did they get that name, it's rubbish" whenever they are mentioned. It's not high in the KC and the Sunshine Band list of catchy names. Just a bit of research finds its quite a clever music industry joke and fits the bands thinking perfectly.

Tenuous Manchester link. In 1979 (idiosyncratic or so he said) Stockport NME journalist Paul Morley wrote a review of The Cure's first album and said it amounted to "No more than insubstantial froth" The Cure then did a John Peel session and changed some of the lyrics of 'Grinding Halt' to include Paul's words and retitled the song "Desperate journalist in ongoing meaningful review situation" Most of Paul's words do have more letters than a Welsh train station. When he heard news of the put down, he was out for an afternoon perambulation around Reddish Vale Country Park.

Tonight, Jo Bevan (vocals) Rob (guitar) Simon (bass) and the aptly named Caz Hellbent (what a powerful drummer she is!) seem even more embittered than ever. By their own admission they much prefer playing on the continent "You get treated so much better in Germany and Austria than you do in the UK" On gig promoters "You only see them once 'Here's your beers' and then they disappear"

Jo has a great voice and on occasion a fearsome attitude. Tonight, she seems close to boiling right over. There is a particularly venomous "Why are you so boring?" which seemed to be directed at a bloke at the bar who mimicked one of her trademark yelps Lots of local musical references mostly to The Chameleons, Smiths and New Order and an angry Jo seems hellbent on strangling herself with that microphone lead. A move even Morrissey would stray away from. On the album's inner sleeve is a quote from Virginia Woolf "Nothing thicker than a knife's blade separates happiness from melancholy"

Caz's punchy drumming is brilliantly augmented by strident guitar. Sometimes rock, sometimes indie, sometime jangly. Powerful but with an almost detached air tonight. As a post punk band not sure how the attitude would have gone down at The Electric Circus in 1977. They might have been greeted with more than applause. Was there something amiss tonight?

For the encore, guitarist Rob emerged clutching a wad of notes "We are OK now, we've been paid" Still not sure if he was joking or not. Another of Jo's laments is the lack of working class in the industry, and the dominance of art school indie. Don't think this could be levelled at Klondyke Club favourites, the thunderous local support band LIINES. Them ramshackle Soup Kitchen toilets nearly unhinged. There was a great moment when I'm pretty sure it was singer Zoe's mum made the most angelic and graceful entry down them dodgy stairs. Again, going on looks alone she was spotted by her other daughter and dragged into an all-female mosh pit, never to be seen again.

Top Tunes: "Never there " LIINES "Be kind" Desperate Journalist

Bank cards and beer festivals

What a joy to have an old mate J who now owns his own brewery (Manchester Union Lager). Well if joy is 90% jealousy. He even had his own lager festival this year. A full weekend of Hedonism. You bought beer tokens on the door. £4 a token and each token bought one of the huge choice of lagers. Security was tight, the bouncer said, "Have you got a ticket?" "I'm a mate of Jamie's" Exasperated "Everybody's a mate of Jamie's. See that woman there" She said, "How do you know Jamie?" "Err football and that. How do you know him?" "I'm his wife" Always important to make a good first impression. On the Saturday night as well as the Manchester Union, managed a Devin the Dudes, an Innis and Gunn, a Gunmetal and a Running with Sceptres, and while my mates wife wasn't looking we snaffled a couple of Rock Bottom 2019, 8%, the deep thinkers brew, or at least you thought you were. The braincell was in full retreat.

A couple of friends who were also with their better halves grudgingly left me their spare tokens. One who was a renowned nutcase in the 1990s approached and said maturely "You coming back tomorrow, we have to go now" The wife had her head slightly tilted to one side and a smile that seemed to say "Are you still staring at women on buses?" Marital bliss. The next day everything seemed to go swimmingly, and me and a Wythenshawe mate patiently made our way through half the pumps on the other side of Campfield Market. Vaguely I remember trying and failing to use my debit card at

Spinningfields" Doh, blocked! but it only became urgent when trying to get some money for work on the Monday. Ringing from a cashpoint on Mosley St, the Lloyds bank lady had to stick to her script without deviating. "I think my card was blocked last night" "Well can you remember the pattern of numbers?" "I can't even remember one of the numbers, I was at a beer festival yesterday" Mild giggling away from the phone, I think she is coming with us next year.

Big Thief

Led by the enigmatic Adrianne Lenker, Big Thief are a fantastic band. Their songs are beautiful, often difficult and painfully honest. The first two albums, Masterpiece and Capacity were released quite close together, both are unmistakeably Adrianne's work but somehow strangely different.

As a child, her and her siblings were brought up in a cult before their parents became mortified by what was unfolding in front of them (a bit like a season ticket at OT) and took them away. The family travelled the States in a van and the kids received no formal education. Adrianne didn't get to celebrate a Christmas until she was 8 years old and on the road. Throw in a blow to the head from a metal spike that fell from a tree house and this might go some way to explain her different slant on life.

A family with plenty of time to think. Adrianne recalls the story when at the age of 12 her sister had posed and answered the question "Why are people so keen to lie on a beach on holiday?" "Because it's the only chance they get to have a connection with the planet they live on" Wow. If only the Gallagher's had had a 12-year-old sister.

Genuinely heartfelt lyrics trying to make sense of her past. Traumatic but cathartic. The band were careful not to ruin things, their playing was almost careful. Adrianne's voice at times faded to no more than a whisper. She achieved the impossible, an intimate gig in the vast cowshed of Academy 2. Almost embarrassed by the hush she had created by baring her soul she whispered to the crowd "I hardly know you"

Top Tunes: "Shark Smile" "Mythological Beauty" "Masterpiece"
Big Thief

What was happening in Big Hands later it was like Pwllheli
Caravan Park on a Bank Holiday. Elvis's 'Burning Love' came on
to some form of choreographed Rusholme line dancing on both
sides of the bar. Stop this now.

Early in 2019 Adrianne played a solo gig to a hushed crowd at
YES, her solo songs are just as mesmerising. Without Buck
tonight her own brilliant guitar work is highlighted. It is the
complexity of the lyrics though that leaves everyone awestruck.
You could hear a pin drop between songs, total respect, until one
voice that sounded just like Iain Duncan Smith broke the silence
"You are so brilliant. Please don't stop" Grown men and women
winced in their boots. Adrianne retained her cool and re-assured
her wannabe paramour that she was going nowhere soon.

Top Tune "10 miles" Adrianne Lenker

Big thief

Bill Ryder Jones

Well when they come over for a visit, they like to let you know they are here. Bill Ryder-Jones (The Coral) was playing the Dancehouse Theatre and he had brought all his extended scouse family with him. I hadn't understood so little at a gig since Gwenno decided to talk in a mix of Cornish, Welsh and alien at the Band on the Wall.

Huge problems here if you arrived a little late. Dancehouse had removed all the lower seating and the front steps had quickly filled up. The top area had been kept seated for Merseyside royalty. That left only the flat landing between the exit doors and the few yards behind that for the rest of us. A shocking viewpoint. The diminutive woman next to me was stood behind a giant and spent the whole gig staring into his coat pockets. I did ask her at one time "Have you seen him yet" A shake of the head. I think I caught a glimpse of Bill twice.

Scouse Bill decided to get everyone on board after a giddy, chaotic start. This included him breaking up a full on domestic that had come close to blows on two occasions. "Do you mind packing it in, you're ruining the intro" To calm everyone down he threw in one of his favourite stories. A woman he had romanced in the 'Pool had told him that if he let her give him a moon tattoo it would cement their love forever "I bet you there's another twenty divees walking round Liverpool city centre with the same tattoo" Mild mayhem. From then on, he was in full control.

My excuse for being late and ending up on the blind landing was that I had been in Chimaek. This is the small but bustling Korean restaurant on Hulme St at the side of the Dancehouse. If this is authentic Korean dining, I want to visit Seoul. An air of mild confusion hovered as the K-Pop played. Like new venue YES, they give you a little fob that vibrates and lights up when your food is ready. Great entertainment when three start flashing together. You can write your views on post it notes and stick them on the wall. After twenty minutes waiting and one pint of Asahi was going to stick one up with "Help I'm starving on it" I only wanted a chicken wrap.

For those having the Army Stew or any of the stickier chicken dishes, they give you blue latex gloves to keep the hands clean but that doesn't stop you getting it all over your face. Great place for a first date. What a happy atmosphere though. The Korean youngsters opposite were on the Soju (apparently the world's most popular alcoholic drink, having taken over from Ayingerbrau) and seemed in a state of delirious oblivion. I'm definitely going to go back for some more Korean pop, Soju and latex gloves.

Top Tune: "Wild Swans" Bill Ryder-Jones

No hiding place...

In May 2019, came a fully seated Dancehouse gig where many might have wanted to take cover on the stairs. Jerry Sadowitz ruthlessly critiquing modern society's hypocrisy or something close to that. No modern-day icon or James Corden was safe. Brutally funny. Luckily, I had four lads next to me and one in front who were in tears of laughter, so important at a comedy gig. The last time I had seen Jerry it was many years ago on a first date with a woman from Mayo. She sat bewildered throughout and not long later went home to Achill Island for good.

Get the bus...

They were all saying it. Now that the tram system seemed to have cornered the market in the walking dead and raving roving weirdos, the bus service was now the preferred late-night transport home. Unconvinced I got on the 43 at The Refuge. Would the 45-minute trip back to Wythenshawe be incident free. The peace didn't even last 45 seconds. Those first few seconds seemed fine. I sat near the stairs and glanced down the bus to see if there was a better seat. Spotting a free seat near the back I went to head back there. Just as I did the woman on the seat in front burst into song at the top of her voice. A one-woman toothless flash choir. A very original lispy vodka infused rendition of Bowies "Life on Mars" followed. Not sure if the rest of the passengers had already been treated to the early verses but we were at "Take a look at the lawman beating up the wrong guy" Mesmerising.

Looking like Susan Boyle in a leather mini after a heavy night, she trudged off in Rusholme to no applause but much relief. She stopped briefly and told the driver in an almost sinister voice "I trust you with my life me" He didn't even look a bit like Simon

Cowell and still looked part bewildered, part terrified 40 minutes later. On this evidence Rusholme hasn't got talent. 0/5 and bus drivers need a pay rise.

Blackthorn Festival

A wonderful festival set in the beautiful surrounds of White Bottom Farm, Etherow Park, Romiley. Lots of young bands take their hugely enthusiastic first steps here in this stunning location and what a joyful place to start.

Today most of the young upstarts are to be found on the Paddock stage and have brought a range of supporters. Delights have a cool following, Dear Caroline a too cool for skool following and Dirty Laces one escaped lunatic "I'm the ex-bassist me" Ex said it all. On the Meadow stage also hugely enjoyed Queen Cult after managing to escape the ex-bassist.

My favourite character though had to be the fantastically named rock god, Ben le Jeune of Creature Comforts. Ben gives it the full-on rock posturings like he was playing Wembley Stadium. Iggy Pop's brother in a denim jacket. He then totally misjudges a leap off stage and nearly wipes out an unsuspecting female photographer who hadn't seen him coming. Bounced back on his feet like he'd survived a Vic Reeves frying pan and was back on stage barely missing a quaver. Rock legend.

So easy to meet new friends here. Three years ago, I met the parents of Sly Antics on the 384 bus to Etherow. Excited and proud as punch, as we walked round the lake to the venue, they told me all about their hometown of Hebden Bridge "Everyone is either an actor or in a band" Difficult work in Hebden job centre. Saw the Antic's dad recently at their gig in the Anthony Burgess Centre and touring looked like it was beginning to take its toll. Long leather coat, unshaven, pint in hand, singing along with angst ridden expression, he was feeling it deeply. The road to the top can be tough for mum and dad. On stage the band were bouncing around having a great time.

The following year I travelled to Romiley by train and chatted to a lad with a guitar strapped to his back and his girlfriend. They were unsure of the layout of the station when we got off. He was the bassist from Ist Ist and said the singer's mum was picking them up "We'd give you a lift, but I think the car is full" He was right she turned up in something no bigger than a bumper car. Rock n roll. These days the Ists might stretch to a limo.

There are also plenty of cases of mistaken identity. Walking from Paddock to Meadow stage got a slap on the back from a huge grinning Cockney fella "Lyerr are one of my bands, I've got another three on later. What are you doing here mate anyway?" Not a single clue who he was. Then inadvertently insulted the huge Indian guy in a green turban on the kebab stall when he said, "What you having our kid?" in a voice Terry Christian couldn't have copied "Top accent mate" "Should be I've lived here 62 years" Apologies Stockport Sikhs.

At the bar chatted with a band called Big Slur. That festival feeling when you peak too soon, and a gradual decline becomes a careering downhill dash. Almost definitely they had picked the mushrooms for the morning omelette. They had travelled a long way to see their hero Pete Doherty. Originally from the Isle of Wight they were now on the run or seeking greener grass in Vietnam. The guitarist had the best head of rock hair, John Lennon sunglasses and even in the searing heat a huge baggy red mohair jumper. Slowly they visibly wilted and drifted off back to their tent. Not sure either they or Pete made the headline slot, I'd gone for the last 384. The Vietnam bus was probably cancelled.

Got the chance to watch the hugely tipped Blinders with two mad friends from Oldham, Helen and Angela. Helen was bonkers with what appeared to be a Wonder Woman brooch stuck to her forehead and lights in her hair. Angela was the more sensible, but her Lancastrian accent was by far the stronger. They told the story of how they'd overdone it here last year and missed all the transport home. Hitching around the lake they were picked up by a swinging couple. Random cruising swingers in Romiley, who'd have thought it? The woman asked Angela straight out if they were lesbians! When she said no, the swinger said, "How do you know you're not a lesbian?" Fantastic to have that story recounted in a Victoria Wood accent.

They were having a great time tonight despite me telling them I thought Oasis were garbage. Helen put her fingers in her ears in mock horror and spun round "I'm not listening. I'm not listening"

As darkness closed in, with the lights in her hair, wherever they went to dance you could still spot her, bobbing about like a buoy in a murky sea.

Got to see local heroine Findlay play and she was outstanding. In a World Cup year her joy at playing on home turf was only momentarily disturbed by her keyboard player capturing the mood of the nation and playing an impromptu "Findlay's coming home"

Top Tunes: "Waste my time" Findlay "Dear Caroline" Dear Caroline "Hear you call" Courtyards "Naked Heart" Delights

If you are new to Blackthorn the setting of the sun can be quite alarming. The atmosphere changes in an instant as lone malevolent but mostly harmless Shrek like figures arrive, probably from caves in the hills above. All of them seem to have some grudge with life. 2019's star turn was a self-confessed detectorist and Ed Balls lookalike from Anglesey who had married a Stockport girl 24 years ago. No sign of the wife tonight he had probably rolled a boulder over the cave entrance.

A very individual line of patter that left the barmaid near to tears. He was arguing the toss over his beer token being £4 and the pint he'd ordered being £4.50. Needing the toilet, he refused to leave his 2/3 empty pint pot (deposit £1) with me as "you look dodgy and you might spike it" Quark, Strangeness, No charm. Sadly, he did return from the latrines "Life is too short. Why work for a living when you can search for treasure?" Sounds a good argument. "Have you heard of Romelu and Rebus, the founders of Rome?" "Kind of" He then pulled up a photo of a vase he said he had unearthed that depicted the brothers. He then changed in an instant told the bemused bar staff I was a copper and cleared off to polish his vases. "Honey I'm home"

Away from Ed, some great one liners today. Had arrived at the bar precisely at mid-day at the same time as two women. About 8 hours later the three of us were back there again, just as Sam of Republica strangled a note in Drop dead Gorgeous. I saw one of the women wince and said to her "Any highlights so far today?" "No not really" Harsh! You have to be in that festival mood.

Loved The Elephant Trees singer describing their sound as "music for a depressed kid's disco" Satyr Play pleading with their followers" If you liked the last single would you buy it and help us on our journey to get out of Moston"

So many bands had loved ones and close friends with them offering vocal support. Lancastrian band, The Lathums frontman who is in the vanguard of the lead singers in glasses movement had to cope with the unusual disruption of a dog barking along to one song. Gazing out at the rural paradise from the 42's stage he said, "It's lovely here isn't it?" "Not as lovely as Wigan" came a voice from stage left.

Both PROSE and Afghan Sand Gang looked like they had really indulged in the festival spirit before taking the stage prompting one voice to ask the Afghan's vocalist "Do you know where you are Paddy?" A moment's thought "Does anybody know?"

Top Tunes: Callow Youth "Did it really matter" The Lathums "The Great Escape" Elephant Trees "90 Degrees" Brix and the Extricated "Dead beat Descendant" PROSE "Caravan" The K's "Glass Towns"

Brian Jonestown Massacre at the Leadmill

BJM had been a band I had striven to see for two almost two decades without success. Something had always come between us. Finally, a chance in 2018 to see them and throw in a visit to a place I'd always wanted to go. A place of rock legend. The Leadmill in Sheffield town centre.

You can't beat a midweek trip to another civilisation. It's the kind of thing that Attenborough has thrived on for years, but only rarely has he ever had to put up with Northern Rail. A bewildering batch of announcements and platform changes left passengers bruised and befuddled. "Sheffield passengers please board the front train on platform 1"which had Hull on it "The Hull service has been cancelled due to staff shortages" "Chris Grayling knows what he's doing" "Sheffield passengers please board the train that is arriving on platform 2" "Passengers on platform 2 do not board the Sheffield train if you are alighting before New Mills, go to platform 5" "Andy Burnham's eyebrows are lovely" and so it went on. Forty minutes later our train departed with punch-drunk passengers not knowing or caring where it was going. Northern Powerhouse.

I chatted to a Chinley couple who had been out for a meal in town to celebrate her 70th birthday. They were Dr Feelgood and Colne Blues Festival fans and for her birthday she had had her hair infused with pink. Lovely people but with the strange habit of the first words of the sentence being completely intelligible but the last words all condensed into one. This brand of quirkiness would resurface later in Sheffield. "If you like your music get yerself to see Everley Pregnant Brothers lad" "They've a song called 'No oven no pie' epitomyoftsheffieldhumour" Did get to listen them when I got home and must say I preferred the Kings of Leon cover "Me chip pan's on fire" Who knew Sheffield had its own brand of humour?

In Sheffield couldn't resist a cure all hot n sour soup before checking into the hotel. The waitress said, "You wan Chinese beer with that?" "Too right yeah" Turned out to be Tsingtao brewed in Halewood, in the western province of Merseyside.

The gig was fantastic, so worth the wait. A hugely intoxicated unruly crowd included 3 fallers. One went sprawling spectacularly at the bar. What to do? Pick him up or utilise the space. A drinker's dilemma. I moved quickly and just shouted "2 Somersby please"

Some consternation at curtain call, one of our Jonestown heroes was missing. Suddenly he was rushed from the crowd to the stage door by bouncers like security men rushing an American President away from danger. Stage door pulled open, him flung through it, then door slammed again. Wasn't close enough to see but really hope it was mad tambourinist Joel. A fantastic guitar band, how the Gallagher's could have done with this panache. Singer Anton continued his edgy relationship throughout with the vociferous crowd, at one time telling them "Shut the fuck up, I'm driving this car. You're just in the baby seat" An exhilarating night only let down by the Sheffield after party.

I'd had some fine Belgian beer pre gig in The Head of Steam, but it was long closed when I got back there. Managed a nightcap in The Graduate and she gave directions to one of the worst doners in living memory. Passed flimsily dressed studes queuing for the shockingly still open Tank but just beaten to the counter by 4 roadie looking types who ordered pizza. Pizza in a kebab shop! Unforgivable, that is a criminal offence.

In a cafe next morning, the owner and staff were enthusing over "The funniest thing I've ever seen" One of the women said "It really resonates to the area... it's our Kill a Mocking Bird" (This was no ordinary greasy spoon) Owner Andrew agreed "and it's just full of dark Sheffield humour" What was this masterpiece I asked "It's called The Nap, setintpubuptroad "Eh? Who's it by?" "Ah now you've got me, same fella as wrote play made James Corden famous" "James Corden's famous? Oh no"

Top Tunes "Anemone" Brian Jonestown Massacre
"Chip Pan" Everly Pregnant Brothers

Brussels

Sometimes one sentence can just render you speechless. Eurostar is a great way to travel to and from northern Europe. Security is tight but not overbearing. After a dross game v Anderlecht, was back in Brussels Midi looking for the train home. Due to refurbishment check in had been moved to a different quite cramped area. An earlier train had been delayed but the staff still managed to quite successfully separate the two trainloads.

This wasn't enough to impress a Dublin woman who remained unconvinced she was in the right line "Will you just look at them security fellas doing nothing" 'I think we have to wait till they clear that other train' She was in confessional mode "Mind you, I've got a knife through here twice before. I don't like the skin on apples, so I use it to peel them" Dumbfounded. She was a retired EU secretary popping over to London to visit relatives, or so she said

Brussels is a great place. I had booked an air bnb in Ixelles, near Audrey Hepburn's birthplace. The flat covered one whole floor of a block. It was big enough to house the owners Sohail and wife, their kids and a mysterious American. He politely informed me that house rules required you to remove your shoes when you entered. I asked the correct pronunciation of his name and he said 'Schwale' Needless to say that became Swalesy (after the late great City chairman) when I was stumbling in at 3 am. Strangely Sohail was always up getting a glass of water as I hopped around trying to get my shoes off. Really them monks need to be given more to do than concoct that Tripel Karmeliet. What a brew! Sohail was a great guy, he told me all the best places to visit and was ultra-helpful throughout. After the Arena bomb, he contacted me to say how sad he and his family felt for the victims and the city of Manchester. Lovely fella. Never did see the American but there was a huge pair of Nike basketball boots just inside the door all the time I was there. Student.

Delirium Cafe should be in everybody's top ten places to visit. Located across the alley from the Jeannike Pis statue it spans the full street, 3 floors and 4 bars, or is it the other way around? Apparently, it has over two thousand beers. Now that would be a lifetime achievement.

Starting in the small snug like bar, I sampled a couple of Chimay Tripel White. It was promotion's week and they gave you a big lump of Chimay cheese with each beer. Can you imagine Robinsons doing this?

I sat at the bar with just a handful of others. Barman Davide was very young but had the resigned air of a New Moston landlord who had seen it all before. His English was impeccable having lived in London and he could greet many tourists in their own language but struggled a bit when it came to the Japanese. In one down moment as he cleaned glasses he declared "It really doesn't matter. In a couple of years Brussels will be part of France anyway" Either the cheese or beer was too strong to question this in any coherent manner.

The pub door was open, and I said hello to a group of United fans passing by to see Jeannike's statue. They said they were going into Delirium 2, the larger downstairs bar next door. Davide questioned why I wasn't joining them "Maybe you are a little introverted?" "Yes, and a lot anti-social" Davide "Me too" and an American woman sat at the bar with her husband who had been mute so far said "That makes four of us" The Outcasts. We had a good chat after that.

Finally, I was convinced by old friend Karl (Croydon via Crossacres) to join them in the main bar but not before Davide had asked K "Are you part of an Ultra group?" K "Yep UltraPissheads"

We got drinking with some young American girl students who seemed well schooled in Belgian beers. For reasons unknown Ashley from Tennessee took a real shine to me but then introduced me to the joys of Kwak. To avoid accidents this beer comes in a test tube like glass attached to its own tripod. What a storming drink we had. Ashley disappeared off to the toilet. Next thing I remember was the bearded barman waking me still perched on my high bar stool. Another French sounding lad he was genuinely horrified by my lack of tactical know how. Ashley was nowhere to be seen. Barman arms outstretched eyes wide open in horror "What the f*ck have you done" A four Kwak relationship.

By the time the taxi got me home it was after 3 and to some extent I'd sobered up "Alright Swalesy"

Top Belgian Tunes: not sure what censorship was in place but wherever you went pub, cafe, shop one of these tunes was playing.

"Super Duper Love" Joss Stone "Foundations" Kate Nash "Pack Up" Eliza Doolittle

We can only be thankful they haven't discovered Ed Sheeran yet.

Language Difficulties

In my old workplace I was once taught the workings of a machine by a Polish lad. Quite a complicated piece of gear he left me looking at it and came back later to see if it made any sense. Tomas "Is it clear now?" "I'm not sure, I can't quite get my head around it" He stepped back took a look at the size of my head and then a look at the machine

Bolton and the townships

Had last visited Bolton as a schoolkid. As the turnstiles at the United end were overflowing, we paid into the home sides popular end and were playfully ushered directly back out again by a gang of wild-eyed locals who were dressed like David Hasselhoff and went to the same hair stylist as Rick Parfitt. First impressions. This time there seemed little improvement. Having wrongfully taken a right out of the train station went passed some hostelries at just before opening time. Random locals were stood outside scratching their chins with that "Here we go again. How the hell did I survive last night?" look.

The most famous Boltonian I know of is Peveril stalwart, Mick, who claims his surname isn't Bond. Claiming to work in 'construction', the last four workplaces on his CV are East Timor, The Crimea, Chechnya and Somalia. He has a cap over his umbrella tip and lives at number 006. One time he accidentally turned up in the pub in a bullet proof denim jacket. A man of mystery.

Turned out it was Bolton Food Festival with a few glasses from the Cider Festival thrown in. A great time to visit. Easily found my destination with directions from an ultra-helpful flat cap "If you've gone down the steep hill, you've gone too far"

Taste of Greece Cafe is ace and never to be confused with the one in Wythenshawe, The taste of Grease. Mother and daughter serving and happily chatting away in Greek. The daughter recommended a Mythos (Athens via Scottish and Newcastle) to have with my Greek omelette. A family of Boltonians arrived and way more in the know than me, they all ordered the Yeros. They had just returned from island hopping and were continuing the holiday.

Across the road is the fantastic Ye Old Man and Scythe, the most haunted public house in the country. Dating from 1251, it has only ever had one major refurbishment that somewhat ruined the décor in 1636. Early Enterprise.

Had a couple of decent ciders and the only unworldly things happening seemed to be on the jukebox. Cliff Richard followed by Slipknot. How hard do you have to be to put Cliff on in a downtown Bolton boozer? A couple celebrating a birthday came in and cut straight to the chase. "Where's this ghost then?" Barmaid "Which one?" (The metal fan or the Cliff fan?) The barmaid fixed the woman with a knowing stare "Some people are more susceptible. Apparently, the ladies is full of them" Intriguing. Maybe they don't have enough cubicles. Another pint of Aspalls please.

Wandering around the food stalls later there was a really happy relaxed atmosphere. Bolton Cafe Culture. The Lancastrian landed gentry. Along with the standard meat and potato you could get almost anything in a crust, tapas pie, pulled duck pie, tofu and quinoa with black pudding. Still fashion seems a problem. An endless supply of old boys in blazers with regimental badges and a lad at one stall placing a huge office order, light grey suit and bright red Doc Martens.

As you sweep downhill from Punjabi Appliances the tram rattles right passed shop doorways. You could almost be in Lisbon. Instead this is where the wagon train ends, Rochdale. The long tram journey has much in common with the Trans-Siberian express especially when it passes through the wilderness around Derker and Kingsway Business Park. Sadly, there are no regional accent announcers on the Metro, but didn't she just say, "Next stop will be Sean Crompton Station"? Those who campaigned unsuccessfully to get St Peter's Sq. station rechristened as Emmeline (Pankhurst) know how difficult it is to get a station renamed yet here was one named after the former Wheeltappers and Shunters club chairman's brother. It was only on the way back I noticed it was Shaw-Crompton.

First impressions are what a jovial bunch, what a great sense of humour. They are all doing Vera and Jack Duckworth impressions, until you realise, they really do speak like that. As a town it is a little too close to Yorkshire for comfort. They are not giving much away. The stock answer is "Dunno, I'm not from round here" Somebody must be. Finally found some funky looking local college students "Can you recommend a decent pub round here?" "No"

On the pub search found plenty of plaques to Gracie Fields. First place she sang, first place she played bingo and first place she had her hoover fixed (Punjabi appliances) Had wanted to pay a visit to the much-vaunted Wow Yau Chow Chinese restaurant at the foot of the glacier known as Yorkshire Street. Sadly, recent torrential rain had melted away much of the ice and flooded the restaurant to goldfish bowl level.

Did manage to find a decent pint in The Medicine Tap. A New Zealand pale ale called Ripper and was overjoyed the barman didn't hit me with that question he used on most of the patrons "You with Camra" It still has a certain stigma and roughly translates as "Do you have a train set?" To carry on the frontier town image, the local character with most to say at the bar was dressed like Wyatt Earp.

Found a seat next to a couple of cheese fanatics scouring the lunchtime menu "Do you still have the cheesecake?" Waitress "No, sorry" "Can we have two cheese and onion pies then" (A leap that would have shattered John Shuttleworth. They went back to savoury) Waitress "Anything with that?" "Chips and beans please" You just knew it would have been the same accompaniments if they'd had the cheesecake

Buffalo Bill in Salford

The origins of expressions are normally pretty obscure. What we do know is that sometime in the late 19C, William Frederick Cody (whilst taking a break from stalking buffalo) heard someone say 'There's a right load of cowboys in Salford'

A few years later in 1887 he decided to put it to the test. He packed 180 horses, 18 buffalo, 10 elk, 5 Texan steers, 4 donkeys,

2 deer, 83 cowboys and girls and 97 Native Americans on to his ark, The State of Nebraska and sailed over to the UK. "The Greatest Show on Earth, Buffalo Bill's Wild West Congress of Rough Riders of the World" (It was a big poster, they didn't do acronyms in these days) was a showcase of rodeo skills with re-enactments of battles from the Wild West. After a few trial dates down south in London and Birmingham it found its spiritual home up here on the banks of the Irwell. They stayed in Salford for over five months, playing to vast crowds in an indoor auditorium on the site of what is now the Lowry Outlet.

The Native Americans were part of the Oglala Lakota Sioux who had pummelled General Custer at Little Big Horn. They also featured in the film Dances with Wolves but sadly the sequel Dancing in Ordsall with Chris Eccleston in the Costner role was never made. Locally plenty of reminders of the American visitors abound with street names like Dakota Ave, Buffalo Court and Kansas Ave.

The Red Indian braves mixed well in the community. The Salford girls were well impressed with the warrior's sturdy appearance compared to the local pasty-faced, bandy-legged locals. In return the Oglala lads tired of that same old Pocahontas look were charmed by a bit of Bet Lynch chic. Anybody looking quizzically at their Salford spouse or loved one should ask themselves Do they walk around in their underwear a lot? Are they prone to splashing on haphazard warpaint? Are they able to vault easily on to passing horses? They could be distant relatives of the Salford Sioux. That wild-eyed urchin running alongside the tram at Exchange Quay hollering may just be doing what comes naturally.

After the show's run finished many of the braves were known to have missed the train that was due to take them back to London and the boat home. This was down either to the charms of the local ale or enchanting ladies. What a leaving do that must have been. One of them to miss the boat was Black Elk, the second cousin of Crazy Horse. Sadly, one of Black Elk's duties whilst in Salford was to perform the traditional funeral and burial of Surrounded, a huge 6' 7" brave who died of respiratory disease in his Ordsall tepee. Back home he had been named in the Sioux tradition after the first thing his mother saw when leaving the maternity tent. His full name was Surrounded Bytheenemy. If any Oglala Sioux were born in Salford today, they are more likely to be called Burning Wheelybin or Twelvecans Fosters.

The tour returned in 1903 and this time we know for sure that one of the chiefs, Charging Thunder made his home in the North West. He married another tour member, sharp shooting cowgirl and horse trainer, Josephine. They went on to live in Salford, Darwen (Lancs) and Gorton. Though a proud Native American, Charging wanted to blend easily into society, so he changed his name to George Williams. There are relatives still living in the area though artefacts are few as his bow and arrows went missing on the move from Darwen to Gorton. George had many jobs including imposing cinema usher/bouncer but is best remembered as a mahout at Belle Vue Zoo. The man from the wilderness had retained his rapport with and love of animals.

Bundobust

It has long frustrated UK pollsters and statisticians that although plainly the largest county nothing much happens in Yorkshire. That is apart from losing the War of the Roses and moaning. Moaning about losing the War of the Roses. Attempts to compile a top ten of things from Yorkshire have always ended in failure as no-one could find more than nine. That was until Bundobust came along and crashed straight in at number one.

Their Manchester branch at 61 Piccadilly is accessed by as Jay Rayner (Observer) once said "as unpromising a doorway as you could get. Even for Manchester" He meant it was hidden by scaffolding and next to Subway. Bundobust according to Google Hindi means arrangement. Here the arrangement is between craft beer and Indian street food.

Pretending I knew what I was doing I ordered at the bar. Two main courses and a pint of local award winners, Cloudwater. An expensive eye. The barmaid said sheepishly "That pint is £7.50 you know?" 'Sorry I meant a pint of Squawk please" Phew saved by the Ardwick brewing heroes. A mighty fine pint it was. That must have been a premier cru Cloudwater as you could live a few days on the streets of Mumbai for £7.50

I settled down in one of the bright booths and was rewarded with a congratulatory wink and a "Great choice" from the waitress. An exceptional Golden Tarka Dal and a tasty Paneer and Mushroom Tikka. Didn't tell her I'd had to google what paneer was.

Chatting to the staff we remembered the place as a Chinese Buffet, and a very young waitress informed me "I think it was a nightclub called Legends in the 1980's" "No no Legends was originally where 5th Avenue is. Next to the Old Garratt." This was all ancient history to her she looked stumped.

It was Ash Wednesday, what a great day to go veggie, if only just for the day. The clientele was an interesting mixed bunch. Some uber trendies knocking about but the best was the excited party of exchange students inhabiting the whole bar area. Maybe some were disappointed the English national dish of Chicken Tikka Masala wasn't on the menu. Think the Squawk was getting to me, but the music seemed to veer between ambient jazz and Indian disco and I'm sure in the middle of that, an instrumental citar version of Pharcyde's "Can't keep running away" Strong ale. Hugely enjoyable lunch and as I left, I spotted the same waitress and asked her what she made of the restaurant's review in The Observer. "It was great but that's the people we've had in ever since" I said, "You don't want too many Observer readers in one place at any one time" "I know" she whispered, "They are so pernickety" Perfect! What a great word.

That Yorkshire list in full (1) Bundobust (2) Rhubarb (3) Jess Ennis (4) Def Leppard (5) Yorkshire pudding (6) Harvey Smith (7) ASDA (8) Jelly Babies (9) Cricket (10) Cat's Eyes

Carmody at The Castle

It was a Monday night in May and the lovely Jess Carmody was playing at the Castle Hotel. At the very same time Manchester City were parading themselves round town after breaking all known records in the 2017-18 football season. That meant according to the Evening News at least 100 000 Mancunians would not be buying tickets to see the classy South London songstress. Her mum had warned her of disaster "It's a Monday night...and there is a parade thing"

Support tonight came from the woman with the poshest name in Rochdale, Morgan Harper Jones. Brilliantly funny intros especially one about self-delusion. When she saw an email arrive from an ex-boyfriend she immediately thought "Look at that, after four years he still can't get over me" Instead it was an email he had copied to all contacts. He was skint and was trying to sell a camera.

Morgan is yet another musician who seems to have had a traumatic time at school. She described herself as 'Forgettable' especially to classmate Helen who at first invited her to a swim party and then rescinded it with a smiley face and heart "You are still on the reserve list" Where is this place in Rochdale with a swimming pool? Does she mean canal?

Top performance from Morgan. At the end of the gig I said "You did great. You must be the most famous person in Rochdale" "No, we've got Lisa Stansfield and him The Rochdale Cowboy" "Cyril Smith?"

Carmody was outstanding and charmed a besotted crowd. That lovely voice soared up to the chapel like roof. Her adoring followers were given an absolute treat. The most unaffected rock star you could ever meet. Despite mum's warnings of no blues, she gave a passionate performance. I bought the CD for a fiver, thanked her and said it had been an absolute delight. She did a little bow with hands clasped together in prayer fashion "Thank you so much" Lovely lady a future star. Hope she makes it to the very top and gets her own parade.

Top Tune: "Before you know me" Carmody

Carmody

Cass McCombs

My two favourite strangers I've ever spoken to at a gig were the couple who had used Cass's 'County Line' as their wedding song. Cue "Don't know this one? Whatever happened to 'One day like this'" It just seemed so random and now we all know what county lines are, really hope it's still a good memory.

Way back in 2003, John Peel had called Cass 'unobtrusively brilliant' To this day people are still debating whether it was a compliment. Cass once declared on one of his more jovial days that his tombstone should read 'Home at last' Quite catchy and cheap. A really prolific songwriter, back home he has been labelled the American Morrissey "Genius storyteller. Glum but humorous" Not that many stories tonight, barely a hello, maybe his glory had been stolen by the support act.

When I saw the line-up for the gig, I thought it included up and coming New Zealand songstress Nadia Reid. Wow what a bill. Turned out it was up and coming Middleton 'broadside balladeer' Jennifer Reid. Manchester's pre-eminent clog dancer and singer of bawdy Industrial Revolution songs.

The look on the audience's faces when she bounded on in what I think was a Paddington Bear jumper was priceless. Had many more got their Reid's mixed up? Was Cass backstage stroking his chin saying, 'I thought she was called Nadia' An act so Northern even Alan Bennett would have taken time to adjust. Jen was once asked why she started performing and she said, "Cos it was better than working in Poundland" She soon had and kept everyone's attention and brought things right up to date with "a little Victorian number" So on trend. Jennifer has played the Croatian Museum of Contemporary Art, the Venice Biennale, Failsworth Festival and I believe once bemused Paxman on Newsnight. Don't ever hang your clogs up Jen.

She references Urmstonian Sam Bamford, the Lancashire Weaver poet in her set. Sam was a devotee of Milton and Tom Paine, and although a radical writer could hardly be considered a threat to society. Incredibly Sam managed to get arrested twice for treason, most famously at Peterloo. He had led a peaceful good-humoured demonstration from Middleton into town to campaign for electoral reform, the repeal of the Corn Laws and the rights of women and the working class. Along with hundreds of others they were attacked by the cavalry. The Manchester Observer was closed down by the ruling classes for using 'Peterloo Massacre' in its headlines. Peterloo being a pun on where the speeches were made St Peter's Fields and the recent Battle of Waterloo. Sam was charged with recruiting an unlawful mob (Langley residents) and spent a year in Lincoln nick. Working class hero.

Another of Jen's favourites is John Collier also known as Tim Bobbin. Tim's surname is still bandied about Manchester today and he has pubs named after him in Urmston and Milnrow. A writer in the Lancashire dialect, epitaph composer, caricaturist (The Lancashire Hogarth) and jobbing pub sign writer. He had a tempestuous relationship with the wife, but they still racked up nine kids. He even wrote the epitaph for his own gravestone

"Here lies Tim and with him Mary, cheek by jowl they never vary. Mary said "That's bobbins that"
Cass was hazy, brooding and brilliant but a little upstaged.
Top Tunes: "Opposite House" Cass McCombs "Holy Law" Nadia Reid "Broadside Ballad Medley "Jennifer Reid

Castle Hotel

Happy vaguely chaotic gigs always stick in the memory. Hannah Ashcroft launched her debut EP in December 2016 during a particularly virulent flu epidemic. Musicians and audience were all suffering. This included an off duty, large bearded felt clothed elf with a raking cough and a depressed air. Band relative on a break from Debenham's zero hours grotto?
The youthful enthusiasm of the bands shone through all the wheezing. They supported each other brilliantly both musically and with hot drinks. James Holt was due to be on first but had gone missing so the night's most experienced performer Jonny Woodhead (a South Island Son) stepped in. An accomplished set. The worries of the promoter were alleviated when James did arrive. Strangely he looked like he had just made his First Communion and been dressed by his grandmother. He apologised for being late but never did explain the half-mast trousers. Some great tunes managed to focus attention on his music.
Caoilfhionn Rose (Keelin to her friends) with her hot Lemsip was immense. Seconds before curtain up she was still tweaking the songs, searching for perfection. When she stepped away from the keyboard, she was faced with an age-old musician's problem. What does someone used to plonking or strumming do with their hands when thrust centre stage? That mug of Lemsip came in handy. Would love to see her sharing the bill with another Manc legend Rioghnach Connolly. That poster would look like an eye test.
Hannah had just returned from Australia where she had recorded the EP. A visible glint in her eye tonight so much so that one of her friends had questioned "Are you OK, these songs are so raunchy" What had happened in Melbourne? We will never know.

Leaving the pub after a great night, met a couple of Keelin's friends on Oldham St, still coughing away. I told them I thought Keelin had won the battle of the bands. They said, "Thank you, you must come and visit us, we all work in Oklahoma" Sadly that's the gift shop on High St, not the American state.
Top Tunes "Borderline" South Island Son "Come out to play "James Holt "Awaken "Caoilfhionn Rose "Nothin' to no one "Hannah Ashcroft (with Jake Spicer)
Didn't see Hannah again till nearly two and a half years later. She supported the splendidly Irish Brigid Mae Power at an engrossed Anthony Burgess Centre. Hannah had survived the solo artist's nightmare of a broken string to give a really accomplished set. She then even did a stint as barmaid during the interval. I told her I had seen her play before at a Manchester showcase at The Castle years earlier. "Really! That was a long time ago. Who did you go there to see?" Now you couldn't really say one of the others, so I said "You" Immediately a revolving red flashing light appeared on her head with 'Stalker' written on it. I bought her CD but by now had made her so nervous she took it back by accident and walked off with it. I was left with my session IPA and a tentative "Err did I pick the CD up?"
Brigid Mae was brilliant, and she hails from close to where my father was from in Galway. Had a chat with her at the end "Whereabouts was he born?" she asked "Ballinasloe" It is a small town dominated by another Brigid, the huge imposing and frankly terrifying, St Brigid's mental hospital. Brigid Mae said that when they used to go passed this scary dark place on the train her mum would say "You kids best behave or you will end up in there" Irish parenting at its best.
Du Blonde (Beth Jeans Houghton) also tells a great story about her relationship with her mum. Although they have always been and still are incredibly close, when she was young the angelic Beth had overdosed on kids tv and decided to add a little something to her mum's drink. She smiled knowingly and left the room when her mum said, "This coffee tastes funny" It was only when her mum reached under Beth's seat and found a small cup of Fairy Liquid labelled "Poison" that she realised what had happened.

46

Celebrity

Despite being an avowed celebrity chaser, I've never been lucky enough to have met or even seen many celebrities, part from that is Terry Christian, Howard Kendall and Ken Barlow. Paul Mason doesn't count as we had decided he was Michelle le Roux. My only pleasurable encounter came on meeting Sir Bobby and Lady Norma Charlton in the arrival's hall of Munich airport. Me and my mate O had travelled over for a pre-season tournament. Lady N was a great laugh and judge of character "I think these lads are only here for the beer Bobby" I would love to pitch an idea to the BBC, 'Celebrities Homes under the Hammer' Nick Knowles, Andrew Neil, Dom Littlewood and Gloria Hunniford are locked in their own homes and trying to escape whilst you are outside with a wrecking ball.

The past two years though have been a goldmine as I have met two fully-fledged card-carrying celebs. Thanks to my friend Mr G I was once introduced to Lemn Sissay (ex Manchester Uni chancellor, Celebrity Mastermind contestant and poet).

I spotted Lemn on a tram to Media City one day and he had attracted a crowd of adoring TV interns, hyperventilating, fanning themselves looking for an intro. They crowded round him getting off. I tapped him on the shoulder "Hey Lemn how you doing?" Even though he hadn't a single clue who I was, huge smile "Fine man, how are you?" Lemn was looking for a stress busting cig before a meet with BBC execs and didn't have a light. Was expecting 6 lighters to appear from nowhere like in Grease. He stayed for a chat. Classy guy, charm personified.

A couple of years back, me and A went to see writer and radio journalist Miranda Sawyer interviewed by Dave Haslam at Gorilla. An enjoyable funny night and later we bumped into her having a pint at HOME. Had a good conversation about Manchester, a lovely lady. Later I messaged her on Twitter to say "Cheers, I was the one from Wythenshawe" and she gave me the world exclusive "I love Wythenshawe, I learnt to swim at Sharston Baths" Scoop!

The extent of Political Meetings in Manchester

Recently had reason to take a complaint to local MP, Mike Kane MK "City fan are you?" "No" "I am" "So what"

47

Christmas Ska

Not sure what makes ska music so perfect for Christmas. Perhaps just the pure joy it engenders. Neville Staple and his band played a storming gig at Band on the Wall that loosened the roof tiles even more than Santa would have done. This was the original all singing all dancing crowd. Absolutely tremendous night. If you were a skinhead when 'Guns of Navarone' (Skatellites) was first popular, you can still love it now and there's no need to go to the barbers. That's the bald truth. Special mention to Neville's missus Christine for some ebullient dancing.

Some great people watching available tonight. An amazing foursome from Preston. Do you ever look at two couples and think surely they've got that wrong? The two large ones weren't together nor were the two gobby ones. Tinder double date confusion or opposites attract? Small male was also the loudest and criminally boring. Waiting seconds to get served, he started drumming his fingers on the bar and said to his quiet tall friend "I am impatient, it's like when I'm on the golf course" zzz But you haven't really lived until you've heard two Lancastrian's singing at the top of their voices "aye aye aye hugging up a big monkey man"

The Christmas markets were in full swing. They still seem to split the city between festive must see and painful overcrowded rip off. Siding with the latter was one barman at the bar on the edge of Albert Sq. The deposit bandits were hoovering the square for discarded mugs and all seemed to be descending on him. His customer is always right smile was becoming a pained grimace. As he turned to the till to refund even more pound coins, emblazoned on the back of his t-shirt "It's the most wonderful time of the year"

Top Tune "Simmer down" Neville Staple

Schneeman Punsch

Coffee can be much worse than alcohol

A full moon and a thirsty queue at Soup Kitchen before a Jeffrey
Lewis gig. Unfortunately, there is only one barman and the queue
is headed by two men who looked like they had been forcibly
removed from London to work for the BBC in Salford. "Who's
next?" "Can I get a decaf cappuccino?" "Will just check if we've
got decaf" Sighs. Outside the winos of the NQ had been mildly
unhinged by the lunar activity. Police sirens blared. Only mild
mutterings so far in the queue. "Yes, can I get you anything else?"
"Slice of vegan cake please" Then his mate ordered a half of Sup
and the carrot cake and they paid with separate debit cards.
Audible dismay the thirsty customers were ready to join the revolt
on Dale St.
Lecturers aren't all sociopaths but the two in the upmarket coffee
place on Oxford St came mighty close. An elder statesman with a

young colleague. Was the old boy feeling slightly insecure? Prone to hand wringing and a quote from Billy Connolly he tried "Ah but aren't we all slightly ridiculous?" No response from his young protege. Searching for re-assurance "Even I can be ridiculous" No disagreement there so he turned to thoughts of his pupils "At that age students are just forming an ego. The problem is when that ego becomes an entity" Other lecturers are available.

Takk on Tariff St looks a fine establishment, but do they have a door policy that you can't get in without a laptop? Legendary hard-core disco establishment Quaffers used to have a policy where if you arrived without a tie the management would loan you one for the night. Maybe Takk hand out pretend keyboards to tap away on at the window seats if you arrive laptop less.

The always busy North Tea Power is my favourite. Even on a midweek afternoon it can be difficult to find a table. A friendly beard moved slightly and motioned to an empty seat. Settling in I noticed that he too was hugely in the minority. One of the few not hunched over a keyboard. The rest of them looked like the staff of Corrie's Underworld beavering away on their machines.

Whatever happened to the art of conversation? The exception to that rule was sat just next to the counter, dressed in mauve v neck and blue slacks, off duty tax inspector in golf club secretary chic. Sadly, for staff and coffee drinkers it seems he is a regular.

Friendly beard seemed transfixed by his conversation, and once you tuned in you just could not tune out. He could have bored his way through a Swiss Alp.

One of the patient baristas was on only her second shift and was all the way from the Czech Republic. Golfer "So how would you say Moravia then?" A firm "Moorava" He didn't seem impressed by this. Had she got it wrong? Can you imagine working in a cafe in Prague and a local said to you in Czech "How do you say Lancashire then?"

The bearded one was now close to agony. I could hear cracking as his fingers and nails grew longer and hair sprouted on the back of his hands. The young Czech girl was working her socks off polishing everything in sight as far away from Ernie Els as she could. So he turned to her friend who was noisily preparing an order. A pneumatic drill wouldn't have drowned him out. "Oh

Naomi, I can feel those vibrations over here. If I'd known I would have brought in my new coffee grinder just for you" Czech lady returned after wearing out her duster and Martin Boreman spouted to her "So who would have known that Naomi came in one day looking like Cleopatra and she knows more about Cleopatra than even I do?"

All too much for friendly beard whose eyes had now turned full on yellow. I left quickly before he hopped over the tables to his victim.

10/10 for coffee

Checked the internet for NQ headlines the next day "Czech barista returns home" "Was that a werewolf spotted on Tib St?" "Golfer still missing"

Courtney was a punk rocker

Comparisons with legends of other eras are usually a disaster. Phil Jones the new Duncan Edwards, Ray Quinn the new Bruce Forsyth, but Courtney Marie Andrews as the new Joni Mitchell could be the one that best stands the test of time. Great songs, lovely voice.

That Manchester skyline keeps on changing. On the way to the Deaf Institute, you see several building sites where you fear the final product. Pomona Island looking ever like Alcatraz is one, anything owned by mad Monopoly player Gary 'Stick a hotel on it' Neville is another, but the cringingly named Circle Square (old BBC) is the most worrying. Can it really deliver the promised tree lined boulevards and riverside dining? Seems they have abandoned the nature reserve idea.

Big question tonight is what to wear for an alt country/folk night. Will Stratton, a guitarist of great note has a fine voice and a top anecdote or two. A class support act. Will played it safe with a check shirt and then working from front to back at the bar. Two lads also in check shirts, a bloke in a check jacket (dressed in the dark), two women in comfortable shoes and various checks and Rupert Bear. Will can definitely pick those notes and he name checked his all-time guitar hero, Leo Kottke which led to much google failure by the trendies as nobody could spell his name.

Courtney had fallen in love with the Institute's famous wallpaper. She really enjoyed herself and gave a supreme performance. "Hey, I've played Manchester before when I was about 20 and there were about 20 people there. I thought wow, now I've really made it"

She has in fact toured since she was 16 and was writing her own songs years before that as a young punk. It was a helpful friend who suggested maybe her look, complicated arrangements and lyrics might be better suited to another genre. There was a wonderful moment when she went to introduce her band even though the bassist and drummer had left the stage. So instead she picked on the guitarist "To let you know what kind of town he's from, his High School shared a fence with a prison"

When the band returned for a deserved encore, someone had informed Courtney which venue they'd played last time they were here "It's a bit controversial it's not really in Manchester. Chorelton. Dulcimer Chorelton. Anyone here from there?" Quite possibly all of them.

As I was happily deplenishing the venue's Brandy stocks at the bar, met a lovely couple who had hot footed it directly from Green Man and were still in festival mood. They didn't look like they'd been sleeping in a field and the dreaded glamping word cropped up, maybe a tepee with central heating and an aga. We sang Courtney's praises and I told them they must return to see Margaret Glaspy in a couple of weeks. The barman was great and I'm sure he threw in a free one at the end or at least I can't remember paying for it.

A great and late night just managed to get to the chippy as it was closing. Tried a plaintive Oliver Twist like "Anything left?" through the partly open door "Just a sausage" Literally just a sausage and one that had been mentioned in the Doomsday Book. Surely my second freebie of the night. Nope £1.30. Saveloyed. Top Tune "Table for one" Courtney Marie Andrews

One literally that literally gives me a headache to this day. Young Wythenshawe woman on the phone to a friend on the tram "I literally literally have no credit left" Aaaargh. A double literally, this is all too much, what could it mean?

Deap Vally, PINS

Finally got to see local heroines PINS after many years of trying. Something had always cropped up, work, weddings, hangovers, visits to donkey sanctuaries. They were supporting fellow rockers Deap Vally (they don't like too many e's) at a boiling hot, moody Ruby Lounge. Deap Vally, (Lindsay and Julie) we are led to believe met at a crochet class. Think crochet class must mean something else in LA.

It was well worth the wait to see the Salford lasses. It's guitarist Lois's birthday and she gets the full hapless tuneless Happy Birthday from the crowd. Before 'Girls like us' the impossibly glamorous singer Faith scans the crowd looking for some female dancers and finds it's 90% baldies with beards. She finally spots a couple of girlies, jumps down and gleefully bounces around with them. Thunderous and joyful set.

Unexpected second support. A Manchester lad arrives with Polish girlfriend. Something has gone seriously amiss. She storms back to the bar but not without blasting him with a sentence that contains at least 3 'curwa's. While she is gone, he looks like a dog waiting outside the paper shop. When she does return, he pretends he wasn't looking at all. He gets a glass of coke and she has the Red Stripe. After a few gulps, the hair is scrunched up into a masochistically tight bun and she starts head banging to Deap Vally. The only one she rested to was my favourite "Smile More" 'I am happily unhappy man'

Deap Vally had done the Manchester apprenticeship with previous visits to Soup Kitchen and Night and Day. Tonight, singer Lindsay bounces on stage with a booming "Manchester!! How the f*ck are you?" I think I can remember Katherine Jenkins using the very same intro. This is the big hair tour. From the very back of a now heaving Ruby Lounge they look like extras from Dynasty.

For someone brought up on the vocal styling of Finbar Furey it can all get a little too kerrang at times but hugely entertaining it is. Drummer Julie sings the praises of Manchester "It's got everything you could ever need" Except maybe a Kendal's and an 8 lane Regent Rd. I wonder if she had visited the Spice Gardens tonight, which had surely taken a new delivery tonight judging by the number of impromptu nappers.

Her mate Lindsay takes the ultimate leap of faith and throws herself to the mercy of the beards and baldies and crowd surfs a record distance. There's still time for the brilliant raucous one about bees with the whistling solo that everyone tries to join in with, badly. All in all, a triumph, I could yet be converted.

Happily, the Lady of Gdansk was in an exhilarated mood at the end. Manchester lad had weathered the storm and they strolled off arm in arm. Rock chicks eh?

Top Tunes "Oh Lord" PINS "Royal Jelly" Deap Vally

Dears and Japanese Breakfast

The bouncer at Super Furry Animals chatting to his mate "I didn't even think they were good when they were good" Even worse somehow one national music paper described The Dears gig at the Deaf Institute as "A very poor man's Arcade Fire 2/5" At least the bouncer wasn't being employed for his musical judgement. Montreal husband and wife team Murray Lightburn and Natalia Yanchak had formed The Dears in the 1990's, briefly became hugely popular in 2003, edged back into the limelight in 2011 and surfaced again in 2017 at a sold-out DI.

For support they had brought along Canadian friend Lou Canon and Brooklyn's Annie Hart. All three were superb, a pulsating night. The energy bounced back from band to crowd to band. Included was the raucous medley 'Love then hate/Lost in the plot' Brilliant. Not sure where the negative reviewer was stood but right at the back was promoter Chris (Hey! Manchester) beaming with delight.

There was a fantastic moment early in the night. During a xxx version of "Hard to be still" Annie Hart shimmied to the side of the stage in her shiny skin-tight catsuit directly towards one couple. Frisson didn't come near to it, he visibly trembled in his boots, and the wife looked at him in sheer horror. Compose yourself man. Phew. Glad we were further back in the shadows.

Top Tunes "Onward and Downward" "1995" "You and me are a gang of losers" The Dears "Coma "Lou Canon "I don't want your love" Annie Hart

Even before Uber became popular, Northern Rail were experimenting with uncomfortable transport sharing. For the umpteenth time, wrong leaves, crew member gone missing or simply couldn't be bothered had led to the cancellation of the last train. The bus replacement driver wasn't for stopping so up yours if you lived in Burnage, Didsbury, Gatley, Heald Green. 'Airport only'

This was good news for one family part way through their journey from Glasgow to Tenerife via Manchester. On the packed bus the two teenage daughters were sat near the front, headphoned up. I sat next to mum from Paisley who was in real holiday mood. Either that or hip flask. The boyfriend was sat behind her and was Russian and seemed to speak no English whatsoever. Was this the new Letter to Brezhnev? Do Russian men get emails "Date Paisley women"? As lovely as she was, does he not know there are over 6 million more women than men in Russia? What did he make of Paisley when he first visited? One Paisley website describes it as being in the top 3 chav towns in the UK and the diet consists of Buckfast, Mayfair's, chewing gum and Sunblest. A holiday escape. Bet they had a great time. As we pulled into the airport, my fellow midweek castaways included a lad who'd been at Slow Dive (Albert Hall) a Gatley girl (Dua Lipa, Academy) and a Heald Green couple who'd been at their son's pub (in Littleborough) The famous five, we all piled into a black cab and shared the fare. Ships that passed in the night and cheap as chips.

Lou and Annie had been great support to the Dears. The choice of warm up band has always fascinated me. On Laura Mvula's 'relationship break up tour' she had chosen Jodie Abacus to play warm up and he played a memorable up-tempo set. Joyful cheese to the chalk of Laura's gloom. Thanking the crowd part way through Jodie told us he was from Lewisham. High pitched squeal in the crowd and a female voice shouted "OMG, Lewisham in London? That's where I'm from" If he hadn't been so taken aback, I'm sure he would have replied "No, Lewisham in Mexico"

Laura was preaching to the sisterhood here. The front of the stage became thronged with camera phones and that strange bent arm waving thing. Public enemy number 1 was her ex-boyfriend. It all became a bit Loose Women the musical. Huddled at the bar avoiding all the flack it was all male "I'll just go get another round in"

Contrast Laura's mood to the sheer joy of Michelle Zauner of Japanese Breakfast. All the way from Oregon to our little Soup Kitchen. She was there and absolutely ecstatic when they pinned the SOLD-OUT signs up. Michelle on stage "Musicians eh? We were always the nerds in class. Artists never have a good adolescence. We didn't even graduate. Look at us now with a sold-out gig in Manchester" It was a gem 5/5

Later in the year they played in Eugene, Oregon and she tweeted her joy at playing a gig at a venue where she used to be cloakroom attendant. Music as a means of escape. Not much goes on in Oregon but timber logging.

Top Tunes: "Everybody wants to love you" "Boyish" Japanese Breakfast

Didsbury

There is nowhere quite as Didsbury as The Art of Tea. Burton Rd is making big efforts, but they are simply new money. This tea shop, come book shop, come picture framers on Barlow Moor Rd is where us real luvvies let our hair down.

Thursday afternoon and there is only the comedy wonky seat near the bookshop available, but it gives a top place for all round people watching and ear wiggery.

An old boy on the way in had said "Make sure you say hello to Roscoe" then helpfully added "it rhymes with Moscow" He obviously didn't think I was a rapper. Resident hound Roscoe curled up on a couch is plainly the star of the show here.

I plumped for the strictly working-class meatballs, but they did have some fancy unrecognisable veg with them and the hipster delight of butterbean hummus. The tables are so close together here you feel like joining in your neighbour's conversation, but I didn't lean forward just in case a chair leg fell off.

My ears pricked up when the young darlings next door said they were trying to organise a music festival next year on their farm. Their friend who would help was currently sailing back home from Tahiti via the Galapagos Islands and Chimichurri. Not sure about the last bit that might have been something they ordered. Really hope he was a stowaway. What a delightful couple they seemed.

Staffing was very low key especially in the bookshop. A lad came out carrying a book and asked me how he would go about buying it. At least I think that's what he asked. An accent to put Prince Charles to shame. The book he had his heart set on was Homer's Odyssey, it was a gift for his girlfriend who was sat at the front of the cafe. When he finally presented it to her, she squealed with delight. The way to a Didsbury woman's heart. To think all them years me and my mates bought Didsbury ladies Lambrinis (pints) in a vain attempt to woo them when a paperback would have done the trick.

The farm couple were going their separate ways for the afternoon only. He was seeing her to the tram stop but told the owner before they left he would return if he could reserve a piece of carrot cake "Of course" "Cheers man you are a legend" In this case the use of the word legend can be totally justified.

They were replaced by another pair of Didsbury beautiful people. A kind of 30 shades of grey couple. As in his hair was about 30 years greyer than hers. They dismissed the waiter twice as they perused the menu with almost lecherous glee. Then he asked her in Didsbury's most salacious voice "Are you being good today?" She was but they both went for something slightly risqué. Haloumi for her (great scandal in Cyprus at present as some samples have only 2% goats' cheese) and he had the avocado (New Zealand police have reported a huge rise in avocado rustling. It is now the number two crime behind sheep grooming) Edgy food eroticism in Dids.

Great food, welcoming atmosphere, unusual soundtrack and excellent dog watching.

Top Tune: "Dark Star" The Grateful Dead

Having once had a mangey one bedroom flat in Didsbury my only lasting connection is keeping the same dentist. The last time I visited an old couple joined me waiting for our heads to be drilled. She was very smiley, but he kept his cap firmly pulled down. Looking at the glorious six-foot posh goldfish pool she said "Aw they must get so bored in there" I said "No they've got no memory. Just as they think they are getting bored; they forget about it...like bus drivers" "Oh are you a bus driver?" "No" Slowly the cap seemed to start taking notice. I said, "You'd think they would have an animal in there with really good teeth" Breakthrough he blurted out "Yeah like a piranha, they have teeth...but you could only have one of them"

Amma's heaven

Just down the road from The Art of Tea but most definitely in a different parish is Amma's Canteen serving top quality Indian street food. It takes some cojones (not on the menu) to open a restaurant in a dreary parade of shops, with traditional Manchester potholes outside and over the road from a crematorium.

Stepping inside is like being transported into another world. Happy, helpful staff genuinely pleased to welcome you into their little haven. People have come from far and wide or in the case of the family next to me, St Helens. Most of the patrons though are from the upper echelons of Chorlton society who have braved crossing Sandy Lane for once. A really excited atmosphere and on a chucking it down Wednesday evening every table has a reserved sign on it. I only managed to get in by telling them I was a fast eater and would easily be gone by 19.30. J Hakkas vegan Indian Pale Ale, a roasted okra starter and a chicken dosa the size of a baseball bat. Great stuff. 5/5

Manc Albums (b)

(6) Omnipresent 'Cast of thousands' 2003
(7) Marple baroque pop 'O shudder' 2015
(8) Wiganers 'Silence is easy' 2003
(9) Drewery pop 'It's better to travel' 1987
(10) Wythenshawe stadium rockers 2020 'Build a tower' 2018

Donovan

You know that mobile hairdresser, yes her, who rides through
Wythenshawe on her bike, skirts billowing, like she's auditioning
for Tamara Drewe? For years she has always shouted a cheery
hello. That's nice, I thought. Friend. It was only recently that I
saw her without wheels for the first time. Walking down a full
tram looking for a seat she shouted to me "Hello Donovan, how
are you?" Mildly amused that a load of Benchill people thought I
was called Donovan I said "Err yeah fine thanks" The only
Donovans I've ever known were the '60s folk crooner in the
Paisley shirt and a West Indian lad at school who was cool

enough to carry it off. For my Irish heritage it just doesn't quite fit. Donovan Doonican? No

Just weeks later on a sunny crisp winter's day I was strolling down Peel Hall Rd thinking beautiful day where can I find a decent beer garden? She rode past me on the pavement "Hi Donovan, still cutting hair?" Destroyed, not only does she think I'm called Donovan she thinks I'm a hairdresser. I went home.

Gloom, Doom and Drone

Something is definitely stirring in the musical world. A 2019 report suggests large numbers of people are searching for more experimental and innovative forms of music. Finally, a backlash against Ed Sheeran warbling about a woman from the west of Ireland or the Gallaghers singing about the girlfriend's choice of razor. In its mildest form this has translated into young people listening to slightly discordant jazz, Sons of Kemet, The Comet is Coming and on a gloomier level a surge in popularity for bands like Sing Sinck Sing, a collaboration between Efrim Menuck and Kevin Doria. Are guitar combo bands becoming defunct? Is time up for trad synth outfits? Does innovation necessarily mean subversion?

If music like everything else tends to go in circles, then today's miserabilists can be likened to an early 1970's Curved Air. The next supergroup from Manchester could well be an updated version of The Enid. If Curved Air is where we are at now, sadly that means by 2025 we will have to endure some badly dressed Scots singing a Shang a lang ditty and a chirpy Cockney asking women to hold him close. They will then be obliterated by a short-lived resurgence of punk, which will in turn by blown away by men in blouses from Islington singing about gold.

Efrim Manuel Menuck was a founder member of the more melodic Godspeed You! Black Emperor. Tonight, he and his mate Kev are wowing the Soup Kitchen with their latest long player. From the side of the stage you can see just how apprehensive the crowd look. These are people who have fully prepared themselves for a troubled night, but can they take on the challenge? Did fans used to brace themselves before a Haircut 100 gig "Are you sure you can handle this tonight?" Even pre warned and prepared, by the end of the gig most look like they had just had four wisdom teeth removed unexpectedly and without anaesthetic. Efrim could feel the pain and at one point asked, "Is everyone OK out there?" Not in a 'make some noise' way but more with the genuine concern of a St John's Ambulance man.

At the end Pat a lad who puts himself through many of these raves walked over and said laughingly "I think that just re-arranged all my internal organs. Did you enjoy it?" Still in shock I asked him where outside of a gig you can listen to this music. Co-Op radio don't play it when you are walking down the deli aisle and you would never listen to this at a family BBQ. I did confess to liking the bit that sounded like an air raid warning siren followed by someone moving a stepladder around in a garage (or was that the cellar man moving beer barrels) Pat had been much taken by the support band A-Sun Amissa (not to be confused with A-ha) leading lights of the primal drone movement. They had added to the doom by commissioning a film to play on the backdrop by ultra-happy Finnish filmmakers and undertakers, Chariot of Black Moth. Extraordinary. A hypnotic movie so bleak it made Eraserhead seem like Little House on the Prairie Julia the barmaid who had been serving downstairs had done a swift transfer and was now on the upstairs bar "I just couldn't listen to them anymore "Pat left with a tip "If you thought that was an ordeal, try going to see Lingua Ignota at YES. She can castrate you with a single note" Final word to the old boy who had stood next to me directly in front of the speaker. How his head must have been mangled. As he left, he had an expression of a relieved Bob Harris who had just been rescued from the wilderness "What instruments were they even playing?" Absolutely addictive. Loved it. Went straight home and bought a ticket for Lingua.

Earworms, Pedal Pushers, Psych and Shazam

An Earworm can be almost fatal especially if it lasts a week and is 'Making your mind up' by Bucks Fizz. Even more frustrating if you can't even name that tune. Shaun Keaveney had played a great song on 6music, but I only caught the band's name, Hey Colossus. Didn't know of the band but thought I would easily be able to trace it on YouTube. They have been going for 16 years and have had 11 albums and numerous singles and EP's. No chance. Thankfully they were touring, that will solve it.

Hey Colossus, played Soup Kitchen on a Friday night in July. Even for a weekend night in the NQ the atmosphere tonight was a just strange. In the venue itself it seemed almost borderline hostile. I felt like the unwanted new neighbour at Abigail's party. As much of an outsider as Edward Woodward arriving on that Scottish island in The Wicker Man. Like a mouse making it through the skirting board and finding it was in Cat Cafe on High St. Often wonder do them cats work a shift pattern and then clock out "It's been a grueller" and get the bus home.

Originally, I stood next to a couple modelling matching denim pedal pushers, thick rimmed NHS glasses with various Psych accessories. They must have matching work and gig wardrobes at home. Get in, quick Mr Benn and out. Hypnotised by the pedal pushers found myself staring until I noticed she was staring right back at me. In a 1960's Psych club she would have said to him "Who is that square?" Behind me Roger Moore in safari suit and cravat was dancing away.

Took refuge in my safe area at Soup Kitchen. That dark area between bar and mixing desk. Two lads at the bar asked "Do you know this band? Radio 6 brought us here" "#me too" We are all being controlled to some extent or other. Four songs in they played my tune and I asked the lads "What's this track called?" "No idea" Asked the sound engineer "Couldn't tell you" He was busy on his phone. No play list.

The gig became mesmerising mainly down to the colossal performance by bassist Joe Thompson. Had never seen a band so brilliantly glued together by one member.

Thankfully things got much clearer at the end. An exiled southerner had earlier asked to leave his backpack behind me in the safe area. Could tell he was southern from yards away by his cheque flat cap that screamed it was from Cockney Apparel. He said his name was 'Ileos' that screamed he was definitely not from Crumpsall. When he came back for the bag, he asked what I thought of the gig and told me nearly everyone here knew each other. They weren't being unfriendly they were merely very aware of strangers. They were all part of the non-sinister North West Psych Club. He pointed out the people he knew including the pedal pushers. There followed a conversation that I mostly translated on Google the next day.

For a start Ileos was actually spelt Aeolos. The club were off to a Psych night on Saturday in Liverpool. "We've got friends in Liverpool" "I haven't" I asked if they would all be going to Manchester Psych Festival in August and he said "Courtney Barnett! "in a way a Cockney says Gordon Bennett. "That's not Psych music"

He was keen to teach me a few decent bands though "Look out for a band called Urf, man" "Earth?" "No U-R-F. What about The Hu? That was my favourite recent gig" "The Who?" He meant the hard rocking Mongolian throat singing ensemble. Getting no change from my musical knowledge he was off with a cheery invite to Liverpool. They were a friendly gang after all.

I finished the night with a pint upstairs and the DJ was playing a track by Rochdale electronic giants, Autechre. But what was it called? Went home and put Shazam on my phone the next day. Top Tunes: Hey Colossus "Hop the railings" Autechre "Eutow"

Elizabeth Gaskell

Manchester city council has always seemed averse to publicising our best tourist attractions. If they happen to be in Longsight, you can forget it all together. Roadworks outside Elizabeth Gaskell House have caused plenty of parking problems. One aspiring writer has left a note pinned to a tree for the local traffic warden. Liz G would have been proud of the handwriting. Lovely font. The letter writer congratulated the traffic enforcement officer on their choice of career. Detailed how he would greet him if they ever met and wished a happy new year to his parents. That's if he knew who they were.

Elizabeth Gaskell (nee Stevenson) was born in Chelsea in 1810. After the tragic early death of her mother, Liz was sent up north (aged only 13 months) to be brought up by her aunt in Cheshire. The leafy surrounds of Knutsford would provide her with a setting for her novel, Cranford.It was a further tragedy, the death of her only son from scarlet fever in 1845, that led Elizabeth into her writing career. She agreed with her husband William that the challenge of writing a novel may well be therapeutic. 'Mary Barton, a tale of Manchester life' was published at first anonymously in 1848. Women's emancipation was still in its early days.

Mr Gaskell was the assistant vicar at Cross St Unitarian Church. There is still a chapel on this site despite previous incarnations being destroyed by a Jacobite mob in 1715 and a Luftwaffe bomb in 1940. The present-day Gaskell Room contains plenty of family memorabilia. The frantic expansion of Manchester during the Industrial Revolution had left Cross St and its surrounds looking and smelling atrocious. Appalling working conditions and poverty had set many scholars rushing to pick up the quill and record the devastating deprivation. The differences between rich and poor, employer and employee were to feature in all of Elizabeth's work. In the same year as the Gaskell's son had died, Engels had written of the living hell of the working class. This was no place to bring up a family, the Gaskells moved away from the inner-city grime to the edges of the glamorous sounding Grindlow Marsh, and number 84 Plymouth Grove. Elizabeth at first was more than a little worried about the astronomical rent of £150pa for their new rural idyll. She joked with a friend that as a precaution she had checked out the conditions in the local debtor's gaol. It was her vow to make the lovely house "Give as much pleasure to others as I can "A warmth that is still present to this day.

Over previous decades Manchester had tried to address the problem of educating the uncouth local yokels. The opening of the Royal Manchester Institute in 1823, Mechanics Institute 1825, Manchester Athenaeum 1835, all provided an opportunity for the working class to learn about science and the arts. The Gaskells were firm believers in education for all, not just for those of privilege. In his free time Bill used to lecture at the Manchester Working Man's College.

Early champions of social networking, the family entertained most of the 19c literati at the new house. Today what a joy it is to wander the same rooms as Charles Dickens, Ford Maddox-Brown, Charlotte Bronte, Charles Halle, Beatrix Potter, John Ruskin, Florence Nightingale, Harriet Beecher Stowe. What an I'm a Celebrity that would have made. Since then Longsight has seen less celebrity activity, though some might have got an invite round to John Thaw's or Faisal Islam's for tea.

In 1854 Elizabeth published her third novel, North and South, again dealing with social injustice. Manchester was thinly disguised under the pseudonym, Milton-Northern. It was whilst writing this she fell out with her new editor, a certain Mr C Dickens. Old Charles was not exactly Renaissance man. The working relationship was described as very difficult. Oliver Sexist was a little too keen to alter Elizabeth's text and even wanted to change the book's title. Elizabeth stood her ground. Dickens mused "If I were Mr Gaskell, oh how I would beat her"

Not as populist or raunchy as the Bronte girls, Elizabeth was probably more worldly wise. A Europhile she travelled widely through Europe with her maid. Husband William preferred to holiday in the UK or maybe have a pint down the local with Dickens. This was a prototype Brexit relationship.

After Elizabeth's death in 1865 her two unmarried daughters, Julia and Meta stayed on. In 1878, The Portico wanted a painting of William Gaskell to celebrate his 30 years as library Chairman. The girls chose their friend and local Hulme artist Annie Robinson for the commission. The painting is usually on show in the study, if it is not on loan at Manchester Art Gallery. Annie may well have met her husband Joseph Swynnerton through the Gaskells. His bust of William G is still on show in The Portico. Annie was eventually elected as the first female member of the Royal Academy in 1922. It had taken them so long she was now aged 77. Emancipation had continued at a snail's pace.

Very helpful knowledgeable staff give a fascinating tour of the house, even including a bit of Grieg on the piano to make us feel welcome. Downstairs in the servant's quarters(cafe), the eight ladies of the book club have been joined by a new recruit in a huge red car coat. Looking more like a Welsh prop forward, he breezed in and excitedly asked if they had enjoyed his book suggestion. One of the ladies replied, "Ooh yes, but it's not one we would normally have chosen" Didn't catch the title but looking at him think it might possibly have been Nothing Lasts Forever (Die Hard) Another difficult relationship has begun.

Emblems of Manchester

Manchester is lucky to have two really good emblems associated with the city. Think of poor old Bristol trying to amalgamate the images of a sailor rolling a cheese down a hill after a fleeing Morris Dancer and you can see how complex things can become. The Manchester worker bee looks fantastic on Council regalia, town hall mosaics and can really liven up a rubbish bin. Even as urban graffiti it looks brilliant, maybe not so great as a tattoo but carved into an old log in your front garden in Heaton Chapel, resplendent.

Voted into second as an iconic local image is the Rice and 3 Curries. Again, it doesn't look so good on Council vans and makes a rubbish tattoo. Not quite as tribal as football but some people have great loyalty to where they eat this delicacy. Sometimes it can be down to which cafe their parents first supported. This and That has its fanatics with the knowledge of where to find it handed down over the generations. I have always been drawn back to where I had my very first, Yadgar on Thomas Street. Have been unfaithful at times with visits to Kabana especially when they had pictures of Rooney and Aguero covered with thin sheets of plastic on the walls. This was to stop football fans of either persuasion flicking Karahi lamb at the legends with their spoons. These days the footballers have gone, there is a bona fide menu and crystal-clear water jugs. That's gentrification for you.

The daddy of them all though is still Cafe Marhaba on Back Piccadilly. The last time I visited in August 2019, I ducked in at 11.20am to avoid a torrential rainstorm. The world-weary old boy behind the counter had his back to me deep frying some samosas. As he turned with a sigh you could tell he was thinking 'What are they here already?' He looked like he had seen and heard everything in the world at least three times before. I felt as welcome as Bruce Willis at a Taliban wedding. The missus was much more welcoming and after ordering I settled in the corner with my Irn Bru and waited.

Everyday Back Piccadilly as a street seems like a catwalk for maniacs. A lad in a hi-vis had followed me in and he seemed remarkably sane. Second in not so. A white xxx polo shirt with exactly the same shirt of the size below on top of it. World's worst shoplifter?

He started off in a Geordie accent "Can I just get the hottest curry you've got?" (11.40 am) Double sighing chef "They are all medium hot" This was going to be a long day. By the time the old lad was serving up his rice and 3 medium hot, polo shirts had turned full on Eastern European and shouted in a Bulgarian twang "Whoa. Is that how you do it? I wanted my rice separate" "It's called rice and three curries"

This somehow kicked off Hi-Vis who started loudly complaining about something. Then the door edged open and a bloke crouched over like a drenched Groucho Marx shouted in "I've heard great things about this place" closed the door and shuffled off.

Seen it all before but still dismayed "Any extras with that?" White polo's replied now in a Karachi accent "Onions and some sauce" Don't think the old boy had the will to ask which sauce. Help could have come from two balding brothers who arrived wrapped up in huge oversized bright red Regatta jackets. The third member of staff gave them the thumbs up and asked for confirmation "Two chicken bhunas?" Out of the oversized coat pockets each pulled a sauce bottle. People do have sauce with curry? It is a sauce!

I polished my lamb, spinach, chicken, rice and belting nan bread off, paid up and headed off. I said to the old girl "This road has always been full of lunatics" She smiled knowingly but he looked at me with "Yep and you are probably one as well" written into his tired features. Much to ponder 5 minutes later sat in Mother Macs discussing First Buses timetables, airport parking and Air Malta with two aging tourists from Oldham

Fat White Family

Ever since the gutter press accused Salieri of spreading a nerve agent on young upstart Mozart's harpsichord keys, there have been stories of great jealousies and rivalries in music. Some genuine bitter clashes between rivals, some fabricated for record sales, some family feuds and others who for one reason or another just couldn't stand each other.

The whole of Manchester grieved when Hooky put his song idea back in his man bag and flounced off to the Seven Oaks. The Ramone brothers Johnny and Joey didn't bother talking to each other off stage for a good 20 years. The Everly Brothers said "We've only ever had one argument. It's just that it's lasted 25 years" The Kinks brothers Ray and Dave Davies argument over who was the more talented ended with Ray long jumping onto Dave's 50th birthday cake. There was the Gallagher v Blur handbags. Kurt Cobain fell out with more than Courtney. He couldn't stand Axl. Axl hated Slash. Simon got on Garfunkel's nerves. What rankled Sir Paul? Why did Lennon come before McCartney in the song writing duo? It's a good job John wasn't around to hear The Frog Chorus. Pink Floyd, Led Zep, Black Sabbath all had their wars of words. Dame Elton John has enjoyed laying into many depending on which side of the bed he had hung his syrup on. Elton mused on Madonna after she was voted world's best lip syncher "She dresses like a fairground stripper" What kind of fairs does he go to? Keith Richard had the temerity to say Elton's Lady Di tribute "Candle in the wind" jarred a bit. In response Sir Elt compared Keith to an arthritic monkey. The Stone's Keith once told the press with a wink that Mick was definitely the band's "smallest member" and Jagger never forgave him.

Today the best jousters are three of the best live bands, Sleaford Mods, Fat White Family, and Idles. Though Idles say they have never implied it, the Sleafords accused them of "appropriating a working class voice" Fat White Family weighed in with "Idles are self-neutering middle class boobs" but then told the Sleafords to stop " banging on about sh*t wages and kebabs" They hit back by saying the Fat Whites were a "D-list Moby covers band" To be honest only one of the three is likely to be found eating vegan tapas in a seafront Bristol wine bar but it doesn't make them bad people.

Once furiously anti-establishment Fat White Family say they are much calmer these days. Their own review of their latest LP 'Serfs Up' compared it to a series of Club Tropicana B-sides. It even features a sax, a flute and a gong. Their supporters lapped it up on a gloriously riotous night at the Ritz which celebrated old and new tunes alike. Self-destruction seemed close at hand both on and off stage. Tremendous sleazy edge to the night and the lid only just about stayed on.

The band had formed in 2011, not as a long-term project but just to play a gig in the pub for their mates and hopefully get enough money for the next week's drink and drugs. That pub could well have been The Queens Head in Brixton where they gained notoriety after hanging a banner from a window saying "The bitch is dead" after Thatcher died. Six years later band member Nathan Saodi has slightly upgraded his ambitions for monetary success "I just want to be able to afford a dog with gold teeth" His brother Lias is the band's vocalist. Their parents had divorced when the boys were still at school. Their Yorkshire mother re-marrying a Unionist from Cookstown, Co Tyrone. As half Tyke, half Algerian at a protestant secondary school in NI, Lias recalls a lively relationship with his schoolmates. With the red hand of Ulster on his school blazer he was once asked if he knew the words to The Sash and he replied, "The Franco-German dance combo?" The ensuing black eye helps him remember the DUP and its supporters as 'medieval bigots'

Still they have carried on firing arrows whenever they could. The band once threatening to join ISIS unless Mac de Marco withdrew from music completely. They even managed to take a shot at nice as pie Wolf Alice after they had won an award labelling them as "landfill indie"

The 'Serfs Up' album was written in a 'windowless bunker' in Sheffield far away from the crack of London. Horrifyingly for the band their old haunt The Queens is now a "100% vegan gastropub with animal free beers and food" In their Yorkshire hangout the band said they were now enjoying "climbing mountains instead of doing mountains of coke" Unsurprisingly they've upset plenty on the way up and not all have been impressed by their new clean living image. Crack magazine's review of the latest album said "Each plodding number sinks quickly into tedium. 3/10" Doubt they cared and neither did the ebullient crowd. Life re-affirming joyful gig. They smashed it 10/10

Top Tunes: Fat White Family "I am Mark E Smith" "Whitest boy on the beach"

Flecky the Ghostbuster

As anyone who has visited Castlefield on a summer's night can testify it can be a bit raucous. Tonight, for the Manchester Ghost Tour (ticket price £6.66) 30 of us brave revellers assemble behind mildly deranged tour guide Flecky. Starting at Lock 91 we are whisked through one of the most haunted areas of the city with a mix of fact, fiction and bunkum. Imposing Flecky hasn't held back, dressed all in black, raven coloured rocker's hair flecked with scarlet. Not quite clear where his soundtrack was playing from but Flecky said it was from a musical codpiece, like the Oldham member of Cameo.

The first stop is under the balcony of The Deansgate with the Beetham towering above us. Almost total disinterest from the pub's patrons. Flecky must be a familiar face. Cultural references are varied and many, Ian Simpson, Bjork, Madonna, John Dee, John Byrom, Sir Lancelot, the Platts of Weatherfield, Mick Hucknall and the clap clinic (not his original backing band)

Next to Campfield Market (a one-time Bjork venue) Flecky points out Castlefield House the world's most haunted call centre. It's about time we got our own back for all those PPI calls. John Byrom, poet, freemason, Satanist, coiner of the phrase Tweedledee Tweedledum and English shorthand inventor gets a prolonged review. Flecky somehow manages to compare his debauchery with an early Madonna. Byrom was born in The Wellington pub (Shambles Sq.) and despite everything somehow managed to get buried in the cathedral grounds. That rotten apple didn't bounce far from the tree.

The historic importance of the Platts (of Coronation St) is discussed at length only to be interrupted by a relieved man stumbling from the bushes still unzipped near St John's Gardens. A cheery bit of banter with the tour's 8 well-dressed ladies from Leigh and off he went towards The White Lion.

Outside the gates of MOSI, Flecky points to "Part of the original track of the world's first passenger railway" "No it's not" comes the voice of a security guard the other side of the fence. Moving on quickly. We go passed St John's Sunday School and I believe Gonorrhoea House. At Castlefield comes one story that no security guard was going to question.

Sir Tarquin was an old central Manchester enforcer, a giant of prodigious strength who controlled the old fort. He was no fan of Round Table employees and it was his habit to imprison and torture them. On the tree outside he would hang the vanquished's shields, a bit like Russian football hooligans hanging captured English football flags upside down. Next to the tree Tarquin suspended a vast copper pot with the inscription "Who valueth not his life a whit Let him this magic basin hit"

Though a Northerner, Lancelot had been residing in the Home Counties but had ventured north to rescue Gawain (Gavin) from the evil Sir Carados in Shrewsbury. The slain Carados was Tarquin's brother. On hearing that Tarquin was holding his mate Sir Lionel prisoner and with confidence buoyed, Lancelot rode further north for the grudge match in Mamucium.

He only made it here after recovering from being dosed with an early form of Rohypnol by the gorgeous temptress Morgan Le Fay which ended up with our champion knight waking up in a forest. It can happen to any of us and often does on a Euro away. Hangover and shame gone and guided by a fairer maiden he eventually made it to Manchester.

On seeing the shields including Lionel's hung out to dry, Lancelot flew into a violent temper and shattered the copper pot. A terrible battle raged through the night with the two sirs fighting like bulls.

Lancelot for the honour of the Round Table and Tarquin to avenge his brother's death. On they fought until with his final energy, Lancelot slew the giant and chopped off his head. Still the terror hadn't finished, and Lancelot had to fight off a malevolent dwarf (again see Euro aways) before freeing his mate. The ramparts have stood silent ever since until the arrival of someone from the west with a hunger for a knighthood, Andrew Burnham.

As Lancelot rode out of Manchester, as newly crowned Northern champion, he tossed his rival's head into Hanging Ditch. To this day no child has ever been christened Tarquin in Manchester. It is now the sole preserve of Arsenal fans. In a strange coincidence if you ever go in the wine shop on Hanging Ditch you can always find someone called Lance, Lionel or Gavin.

Surviving mild heckling between Barca and Dukes we made our way back down the canal. Flecky revealed that the so called Manc Pusher could well be the ghost of an old preacher who drowned here centuries ago. A ghostly figure in a dog collar is often seen down here at night. A demonic Dick Emery.

We finish 90 minutes fine entertainment with a pint back at Lock 91. It is revealed that the building is haunted by a child ghost, Peter Bell, grey cap, grey shirt and grey shorts. A bit like him out of AC/DC. Oddly no matter how many times I've been in town since I've never seen anyone entering or leaving Lock 91. Maybe only Flecky has the key.

Soundtrack: "Word Up" Cameo "You don't know what I know" Sam and Dave

Follakzoid at The White Hotel

Despite rave reviews 'it's the best venue since The Electric Circus" had never managed to get to the White Hotel. Finally, I bought a ticket for Chilean psychedelic trance krautrockers, Follakzoid. Leaving it late getting across town, I jumped in a taxi outside the Midland only for the taxi driver to look completely blank. This was beyond his knowledge; he had never heard of the place.

A brawny chap this geezer looked and sounded like he had survived an eastern European uprising or two. Even so he looked quite alarmed when I said "Dickinson street mate, it's not really Salford more Strangeways" I gave him the postcode and we were there in a couple of minutes. He looked vaguely panicked as he looked over his shoulder "This is the post code" "Just let me out here then" "You want to get out here in the Badlands?" To add to his worries my door had jammed, and he had to jump out to release me. Luckily you could hear banging music coming from just the other side of the abandoned gypsy campsite. My friend drove off, no doubt hugely relieved, dreaming about his upbringing in the good old days of the Siege of Sarajevo. Suddenly I found myself with 4 others who also seemed elated to have arrived safely. One lad said, "I have been before but was so pissed never thought I'd find it again" His mate then stood in a pothole only slightly shallower than the one the Vicar of Dibley stood in. Very relaxed door policy (good as I couldn't locate my ticket) and as soon as you were in you could sense this was a crowd of music lovers. Real anticipation and excitement. You could hear a pin drop as everyone listened intently to support band, Triangle Cuts and they got a great reception.

Follakzoid have been described as 'dance music for people who don't dance' Often compared to bands with short names like Gong, Can or Neu! Their own publicity describes their sound as a "non-rational sonic artform" A stated aim on the last album I (the first two were called III and II) was 'to fill longer spaces of time with fewer and fewer elements' Kindred spirits Neu! Also struggled for album titles as their long players were called, Neu!, Neu!2 and Neu!75. They were a spin off from Kraftwerk and not members of the National Education Union. They liked to keep things minimalist and would sometimes play the same chord repeatedly for 10 minutes.

If you can judge a venue by its toilet facilities, then the White Hotel is right up there. The ensuite bathrooms are truly a sight to behold. Hope the lad who fell into the pothole didn't disappear down anything here in Trainspotting style.

The music really does get to you. Slowly evolving, dark rumbling thumping beats unexpectedly interrupted by a shuddering noise. Like being on a truly sinister ghost train.

Usually the band only consists of the two childhood friends, Domingo and Diego but tonight in the pitch black I'm pretty sure there were three of them. On my way back from the bar somehow managed to bump into three shadowy, brooding figures as they marched purposefully towards the stage. Sounding like Basil Fawlty "Sorry. Sorry. Sorry about that"

The stage was lit only by a tiny lantern that eerily seemed to hover at different heights. (Lanky Domingo was holding it on a stick). A great set with none of that clapping nonsense between tunes. Two tracks that lasted exactly 17 minutes each and two of 13 minutes.

My favourite crowd member trampled all over the too cool to dance image and bounced around like he was listening to Born Slippy for the whole night. Happy as a lark he danced by at one stage saying, "I can't find the bar mate" "It's through that little archway on the left" Off he went only to come dancing back without a drink just seconds later.

Fantastic. So industrial I bet Joy Division would have approved. Bone jarring and hypnotic. This definitely wasn't the Hotel California but spookily very few of the punters seemed to leave. Please tell me the White Hotel isn't residential. Not many had parked up nearby. In the surrounding streets the atmosphere was like a very shady away match. What I thought was a mild tiff between a couple over who was fit to drive home was actually a working girl arguing the toss with a punter over his contact less. 10/10 Intense

Food and Drink Festival 2018

Albert Square is such a great place to hold this shindig, it will be greatly missed in years to come while the area is closed for refurbishment. Food, music and Real Ale with a very strong Mancunian theme. Chaat Cart is always a huge favourite and over the course of the festival also sampled a Souvlaki from Couzina, a Salvi's pizza fritte and a crepe from Vive La Crepe.

Was very taken by the awesome Irish Nutter crepe which featured Nutella and Baileys and asked the lad serving if it was a big seller in France. "No idea mate" he said putting his Peterborough

United baseball cap back on. On the last night I thought I was at the back of the queue for a Vesuvius fritte. In fact, the others were merely spectators. Japanese tourists looking on like watching a horror film, as it sizzled away in a vat of hot oil. This was no raw fish supper. I asked if I'd be able to sink 10 Moretti's after it and he said "No, no it's the other way. It's a hangover cure" Neapolitan street food. Hope they have wide pavements in Naples.

A festival finale in the marquee by the brilliant John Bramwell in front of an adoring crowd. These were I am Kloot fanatics from way back when John's hair was a much darker hue. Have his little legs shrunk as well since then? They piled enough stage gear up for him to stand on that it looked like he was balancing on a bonfire of pallets.

The crowd was up for this as much as John. Definitely old sparring partners. The banter bordering on jovial insult. He kept things marginally under his control by issuing the happy threat "Just cos it's a free gig, it doesn't mean I can't have you thrown out"

He mused on his more mature lifestyle now he had left the big city behind for the refuge of leafy Cheshire. Well not quite the leafy bit, Crewe. A different pace of life. He told how his partner's friend always rings her when Crewe is featured on the weather map on Granada Reports "We're on again"

A belting gig. Huge warmth.

Top Tunes: "Proof" "The same deep water as me" John Bramwell After the brilliance of John's jovial free gig, my problem was that I had a ticket for Okkervill River later the same night at Gorilla. At a pricey £22 they had a lot to live up to. Singer Will Sheff loves a bleak lyric or two. When discussing his "Shelter" song Will admitted that for him" It's just easier to be nicer to a pet than yourself" He includes early in the set his dancefloor filler "Famous Tracheotomies" one of the few songs you can enjoy about life saving operations. In amongst the darkness there is hope though and it comes in the form of a superfan. Stood just to the front left of the stage she knows and mimes every lyric with great intensity. Boyfriend ferries her drinks and stands just behind. His expression is more like he is at a Neighbourhood

Watch meeting. Watching her saved the night for me. This clearly meant so much.

Top Tunes: "Pulled up the ribbon" "The dream and the light" Okkervill River

Food Triangle

I loved the restaurant Insolito on Mosley St with its cracking view of Manchester Art Gallery. Maybe a special occasion price but the food was top notch. Had never eaten swordfish before and even tried an Aperol Spritz the preferred beverage of Ed Woodward. Across the road in the gallery before putting one's nose in the trough it's worth seeking out the Joseph Parry painting "Eccles Wakes Ale House Interior" It's a painting of the old Hare and Hounds, on Church St where anti Corn Law meetings brought huge crowds in the 1840s. The Hare and Hounds is now Best Bargains, Eccles specialising in plastic laundry baskets. The painting dates from much earlier than 1840 and carries the tag "When racing and fighting were at an end, to the alehouse each went with sweetheart or friend" Very much as Eccles is to this day, and I'm sure I've met a great granddaughter of that woman smoking a pipe.

Joseph Parry was a painter and decorator in Liverpool, before he moved to Manchester, caught the artistic bug and found fame. Most of the well-known artists of the time were fancy dan Italians or people with van in their names, so Joe was a trailblazer. A local legend by the time of his death in 1826 he had earned the nickname "The Father of Art"

Another local legend Mary Ellen McTague now runs the fine cafe at the Gallery. Despite the awkward queuing "Are you in the queue" "Don't know, are you?" managed to order the pigeon, black pudding, red cabbage and spuds, £9. Luckily for me just seconds after I got my order in, pigeon was scrubbed off the menu blackboard, I'd got the last one. The first recorded case of pigeon shortage in Manchester.

Swordfish and Pigeon are fine for 10 months of the year but in November and December they have to take a backseat to neighbouring Greggs Boulangerie Festive Bake. "Chicken breast with sage and onion stuffing plus diced bacon in a creamy sage sauce with cranberry and red onion relish and sweetened dried cranberries" No wonder Santa needs a sled. 5/5 (453 calories) Sadly, Insolito was soon to bite the dust. Along with Artisan, Rabbit in the Moon and Rosylee it is no more. Surely some big hitter will take up this glorious space soon (if Andy lowers the rates) Greggs on the other hand is still doing well all year round.

Galway: European must-see cities

An impulse visit and it felt free thanks to Brooks Koepka winning the US Open golf at inflated in play odds of 66-1. A place of song, myth and legend especially after a few Guinness in Murphy's Bar on a Sunday afternoon. What a buzz this city has. Surviving Ryanair's shenanigans at Ringway was a bit depressing but not as much as a teenage girl offering me her seat on the bus into Dublin town centre like I was the eldest Rolling Stone. Spirits surged though after stepping off the train in Galway and saw the wonderful old BnB where I was staying. Part of a terrace that was just one year short of it's centenary, behind the tiny bright red door was a Tardis like interior. The lovely landlady had made tea with home-made scones and jam. A real west of Ireland welcome.

The following morning, I booked a marvellous Galway food tour. My companions were families from Chicago and Carlow, two Dublin brothers and an ever-smiling woman from Philadelphia. Fresh crab on designer local bread, Irish sushi featuring parsnip! Local chocolate, oysters, white brandy, poteen, porter and finishing with some Michelin starred fish fingers. The tour guide Goshia really knew her stuff even though even though she was from well east of Connemara, Krakow. Her patter easily exploited my hangover especially when my bottle of water fell through the bottom of the goodie bag. The only memento that survived was a tiny jar of organic mustard.

Philadelphia woman seemed greatly amused by the fact Brooks had paid for the trip, my hangover and my fear of first-time oysters. Later in the tour she felt relaxed enough to say to the group "Anybody not doing anything later? I'm booked on the

River Corrib tour" but nobody seemed to be listening. As the tour finished, I smarmed "Hey what time does that river trip start?" This time it was her that wasn't listening. You say it best when you say nothing at all. She looked like she had just encountered an evil leprechaun. Must try kissing more blarney stones not scones.

The Skeffington Hotel has traditionally been the venue of all first dates in Galway even through years of changes in musical taste. Tonight, it's an old farmer in his 60s who is trying to woo a new partner of similar vintage. No rebel songs tonight. The sight of him helping her on with her cardigan to Frankie Knuckles "The Whistle Song" was memorable.

On the way into The Skeff had noticed the two mischievous bouncers nudging each other. One of them put his arm up to stop me. Looking me in the eyes "How you fixed for the old drink?" (In English 'How many pints have you had?') "Eh, I've only had two pints" Other bouncer "That's not enough" Not Frankie Knuckles fans then.

Always a great town to visit. Next morning, I got to the station early for the train and asked the ticket clerk "Is that the Dublin train?" "Sure, platform number one now" There's only one platform.

Godlee Observatory

"Do you know what fascinates me? Every creature that has walked on this earth has gazed up and saw that same moon" Mandy the ticket clerk at Heald Green station coming over all philosophical while waiting for the new Northern Rail timetable. The Godlee Observatory is that green octagon shaped room that everyone has glanced up at in Umist. It is the home of the Manchester Astronomical Society, a society cloaked in secrecy. Every Thursday they meet behind closed doors in an atmosphere somewhere between Black Books and Third Rock from the Sun. Entering the building is probably harder than transferring to the Space Station. The security turnstile is playing up much to the annoyance of reluctant tour guide M. Three other astronomers are already present, Anthony, Tony and Graham and I have two tour colleagues, a Physics student at Manchester and her friend, originally from Ghana, who is a medical student in London. I make an early error by calling the designated Anthony, Tony and am greeted with a look like I'd said the earth was flat. Dangerous ground but not as bad as the look M got after asking the Ghanaian girl if they have the internet back home.

The man who provided Manchester with this wonderful place was Francis Godlee. He was a southerner who had made the massive cultural switch and moved from London to Swinton in 1881.Here he set about establishing a cotton empire. Extravagantly bearded, he was known as a great character, reticent or aloof at times but a benevolent employer. He built the observatory in 1903 as a gift to his factory employees at a cost of £10 000. Francis was a risk taker, a biker who once triumphed in the Bath-London penny farthing race. A terrible viewing sport especially for short people and any spectator penguins who can keel over watching it.

The Godlee is a fascinating place. A beautiful 34 step Edwardian spiral staircase takes you up to the Observatory. The equipment itself was built by Dublin firm Grubb. It has an 8-inch refractor counterbalanced by a 12-inch reflector. M is still not into his tour guide step yet. He turns down the chance to make any jokes about size or Irish telescopes. The dome's roof was originally designed to be moved by rope and pulley, so it was made from papier mache to make it as light as possible. Somehow it has survived a Luftwaffe blitz and a century's Manchester drizzle.

M tried to up his game. He risked a one liner about once thinking the Milky Way was a chocolate bar but was met with Ghanaian dismay, so he didn't risk the Galaxy follow up. It was so painful we started finishing his sentences. When telling us the fire safety drill he fluffed his lines completely "Assembly point is at the statue thingy" "The Vimto bottle?" Then unforgivably "I got my love for astronomy from watching that late-night BBC programme err" "The Sky at Night?" Head was in the clouds tonight. "Yes, it was presented by..." "Patrick Moore" Like vampires I think astronomers must only come to life after dark. So, what do astronomers do on summer's nights when it stays light so late? A non-scripted lecture on PowerPoint and noctilucent clouds. An event more boring than watching Trooping the Colour. We were locked in and I was furthest from the door. In space nobody can hear you scream. Real friendly bunch though will return when things get darker.

Top Tune: "Northern Lights" Death Cab for Cutie

Gorton

The most probable translation of Gorton from Olde English is muddy field. Today it is best known for that stunning monastery, donkey sanctuary and Bouncing Billy Barker.

A visit to the donkey sanctuary nestled between Wright Robinson and Abbey Hey schools is a bit special and highly recommended. My sister H is a guardian of the wonderfully named Henry Murphy, an Irish immigrant with an eye for the ladies and a stentorian bray. In August 2017 he was one of 22 donkeys housed at Gorton, 19 chaps and 3 ladies. They do fantastic work helping handicapped children and visiting hospices. The proud, hugely engaging, mostly volunteer staff will give you a full biography of all the residents.

Who knew that as a species, the donkey is most closely related to the African Ass and for that reason their coats are not waterproof. Tell that to them farmers in County Kerry. They are partial to a biscuit especially ginger nuts and can live to a fine age. Gorton's oldest resident lived to a grand 56. 12 years longer than Elvis

Next door to the sanctuary is that centre of sporting excellence, Wright Robinson High School. Years ago, they had a team for every sport including water polo even though they didn't have a pool. When they challenged our football entrenched school to a game of cricket a hurried recruitment plan was put into place "Have you ever watched cricket?" "Yep" "You're in" Can't remember the match but know they let our minibus tyres down. All out.

As far as I know the most famous team to ever come out of Gorton was Bouncing Billy Barker and his young protege Tony McCabe. Legend had it Billy could skim across the surface of the Openshaw Canal and then moonwalk back. He could also jump over a horse from a standing start or leap the length of a snooker table from rest. Manchester City Council tried unsuccessfully to get all 3 events included in the 2002 Commonwealth Games. Bill is immortalised in song and a version by The Gorton Tank (live at The Unicorn, High St) is still available. It is not on Spotify. "It's impossible it can't be done cried many a remarker, but now who's heard of Gorton town and Bouncing Billy Barker" The Leonard Cohen version was never released.

His student Tony McCabe once tap danced on Russell Harty's nose (with permission) without causing visible damage. His speciality though was jumping on and off hen's eggs which he memorably demonstrated on Nationwide in 1974. This tour de force can be googled. "The finest moment in the history of British Television. Tony McCabe Ebaumsworld" Sue Lawley looked hypnotised by the sorcery.

Gym and Tonic

Many years after I should have done, I signed up for a gym membership. The horse had not only bolted, the stable had been knocked down and Gary Neville had built flats on it. I had got a real hang up about the onrush of rotundity after a visit to everyone's favourite Gin Palace, Atlas Bar.

The only space on a packed Friday afternoon was at one of the high tables near the bar. The other table was occupied by a svelte blonde in gym gear working on her laptop, probably working out how few calories she'd had this week. I tried to squeeze between the two tables with my large Daffy's (that's a gin) only for the midriff shirt button to snag on the beer belly high table. Left floundering like a sheep caught in a fence.

Why not get a city centre gym membership? Then I could enjoy a light lunch at a favourite haunt after a bit of dry rowing. On my first day I went to Cafe Istanbul quite proud of my efforts. A bit of borek and bottle of Efes for starters. Couldn't resist telling the tall slim waitress. She was so impressed I had taken the plunge but then informed me she makes the gym every working morning, and also goes swimming three times a week. That blew my proposed timetable out of the water. Inadequacy washed over me. Back to the drawing board or in my case the meze platter.

Staying with that part of the world my next work out took me to the iconic Armenian Tavern, on Albert Square. It has been serving hungry punters from this prime spot since 1968 but this was my first visit. Delightful place with great staff, authentic Armenian food and refreshing Pomegranate wine. Really hospitable welcome but don't mess with these boys. Pity the poor PPI refund salesman who got through to the manager's mobile. He most definitely won't ring again.

I had no idea about Armenia's history until I worked a shift with a passionate Turkish nationalist. At the beginning of a 12 hour shift I'd hit him with the conversation starter "PKK. Who are they again?" Half a day later I was an expert on the Ottoman Empire, Cyprus, Syria, imperialism, the assassination of Rio Ferdinand's great uncle and the 'complex' relationship between Turks and Armenians. So, while I was in Armenian Tav, I texted him "Just having a Kaghambov Dolma" Furious face emoji reply.

Just a couple of weeks later I nackered my Achilles tendon in an unrelated incident. This led to 3 months lay on the couch eating chocolate and takeaways and binge-watching Homes under the Hammer. The best laid plans. Would struggle to get through Atlas's front door now.

You awake? Homes under the Hammer is coming on

Heatons

Heaton Moor treats all the other Heaton's, Chapel, Mersey, Norris and Paul with utter contempt. Really the one named after the Coronation St character should get all the kudos. Local galacticos Heaton Norris Rovers formed the mighty Stockport County in 1890.

The whole area forms a massive buffer zone between the urbanites of Manchester and the country folk of Stockport. As such it combines elements of both, friendly but reserved, diverse in parts insular in others. Over the years it has been the birthplace of or housed some real characters.

Albert Pierrepoint "Britain's leading executioner" lived for a while on Mauldeth Rd in Heaton Mersey. From a family of Yorkshire hangmen, he made over 400 appearances at the gallows. A good few of which were later proved to be the result of dodgy verdicts, which VAR wouldn't allow today. In later life Albert became a pub landlord but quit because he couldn't stand the gallows humour. In his memoirs he came out strongly against the death penalty. It was only a day job.

Fred Karno, the inventor of the slapstick custard pie in the face, married a Heaton's girl and lived there for some years. His name became synonymous with anything comically chaotic, a sort of early Chris Grayling.

Joan Bakewell became a leading light of the feminist movement after grabbing Frank Muir by the bow tie when he called her 'The thinking man's crumpet' on Call my Bluff. Joan lived on Hooley Range, just off Heaton Moor Rd. Mani from the Stone Roses made his home here and there is even a local hobbit, Merry (Dominic Monaghan)

In April 1970, a young musician who had recently won the Ivor Novello award, appeared at local hip joint, Poco a Poco supporting Barclay James Harvest. David Bowie went on to bigger venues, The Poco became The Hind's Head.

La Cantina, on the old Damson site, opposite the Moor Top serves outstanding tapas. Estofado de pollo, chorizo y judias. Chicken stew with broad beans and chorizo is worth the visit alone. Chuck in a bottle or so of Er Boqueron (the beer named after an anchovy) and a Vones gin and tonic. Perfect lunch. 5/5

Hipsters in retreat

What a fate is befalling the indigenous NQ hipster driven to the point of extinction by invaders. Much in the same way that the red squirrel is being hounded out by the grey, the bearded and bangled ones seem to be in full retreat from aggressive intruders. Yes, I'm talking about him who looks like Noel Edmonds in his ironic retro striped shirt and his mate who looks like a leprechaun in a pork pie hat. No way these two know their goji berries from their baked beans. The native hipster looks embattled. Beards are looking scratchy, vintage clobber threadbare. The nu-hipster is on the attack and they have financial backing from mum and dad. (BOMAD)

Attenborough could make a documentary about our heroes' plight. Their flight across Great Ancoats street has proved more difficult than was thought. If they head further east to the townships of Cheetham Hill, Collyhurst, Miles Platting and Beswick they are more likely to end up in a big cooking pot. To the south the Chorlton reservation is full. If this was in Africa, a special squad would be formed of people who used to hate the Real Hipster but now on seeing their rapid decline are determined to save them. Sadly, Lord Burnham is unlikely to impose emergency measures to rescue our friends. Bomads are worth too much.

Indie strongholds are being bulldozed by corporate monsters. Gary Neville cruising the streets in a blacked-out limo looking for something, anything to develop. Cafes and pubs are full of newbies. Even Kabana is now gentrified and is definitely using recipes.

Tonight, it's the launch of Honeyfeet's album at Gorilla. A joyous party. These are the NQ's favourite band. Dangerously both tribes are present. Pork pie hat's mob have marked their territory to the left of the stage and created their own problem. Only time to squeal and hug about 80% of people heading passed to the toilets. This causes confusion on the way back "Have we already hugged?" The trad hipsters arrive late to find their space occupied. Dismayed they go elsewhere, one even mumbling "Would be different if you wanted to see the band" Thus letting everyone know they had seen them many, many times before when they were unknown.

Honeyfeet's ebullient singer Rioconnaigh Connolly is on great form, swigging away on a bottle and joking with the crowd. Always happy despite having been kept down at infant school for not being able to spell her name, allegedly. Rumour has it that Abz from Five suffered the same fate.

Raina (to her friends) has a ribald patter between songs but luckily her Irish accent is deeper than Lough Derg, so a lot of it remains a mystery. Some militant feminist jibes go down great. One song is introduced with what I thought was "This is for all of you with a neurosis" Wild cheering. Only when that 3 second translation app in the head kicked in, I realised she said uterus not neurosis.

Brilliant performances, the drummer had an absolute blinder, so it was a bit of a damp squib when they trooped off without encore under management curfew. Raina wasn't trooping anywhere and was left clinging to the mic stand "I can't move" That was definitely not cold tea in that Jack Daniels bottle.

Top Tune: "Sinner "Honeyfeet

Hispi

An aborted visit to the well touted Japanese restaurant Kyoto on Copson St, Withington. According to Google it was open, but the ramshackle shutters were down and there were no signs of life. Had they done a flit? Looked around to ask but this is not Withington's most salubrious boulevard. The people outside the nearby cafe looked even more ramshackle. Good excuse to head back to Dids.

Hispi on School Lane, top class 3 course lunch for £19, a fantastic bargain. That's if you don't double that on beer and wine. Mackerel, beef skirt and doughnuts were my three choices and it could well have been the best meal I've ever had. Only two other customers, an Altrincham couple. It got distinctly uncomfortable later (but a great watch) when all of his credit cards failed, and they had to scrape £38 in cash from trench coat pockets and the bottom of her handbag.

I had already established my credentials as definitely not a food blogger. The mackerel starter came with some delicious exotic tasting fruity squares. I called the waitress over "Wow that's lovely. What are them squares?" Stood next to me like a friendly infant school dinner lady she said sympathetically "That's apple. Pickled apple" (Translation: Gump, get them eaten)

Outside in the sunshine Hispi's travelling knife sharpener was having a great time. What a job, like an old blacksmith doing his bit. Whilst I polished off the beef skirt, I asked the waitress who all the names were on the huge mirror. Originally the restaurant was part crowd funded. If you made a contribution you could have your name engraved on the glass or they could send a chef and server round to your house to rustle up your tea. Knife sharpener extra. Great idea.

Egged on by the waitress I ordered the doughnuts, ice cream and chocolate sauce with Homer Simpson like glee. Paid with two bedraggled twenty-pound notes (up yours Alty) and cleared off telling my bemused new friend "That was the best thing ever. Can I come back tomorrow" 5/5?

Hiss Golden Messenger

A week previously at the Phoebe Bridgers' gig I had spoken to the bookings manager for Barrowlands (Glasgow). I told him I was going to see Hiss Golden Messenger and he pulled a face like John Torode confronted with a pot noodle.

It definitely wasn't him though confronting a benign group of alt folk followers in the doorway of the Deaf Institute before the gig. As I got there the locally based charmer was just finishing his rant with the random "and anyway I'm not from Preston me, I was born and bred in Derby" What looked like a dozen or so members of a Lancashire Folk Club carried on up the stairs dumbstruck. I went to the downstairs bar and told the barman "There's a proper idiot out there heckling the queue" He said "Oh no, I know him. He comes in here, nicks all the free papers and tries to sell them to passers-by" Enterprise culture.

A comfortably sweat shirted, orderly crowd but with a hint of social awkwardness. Don't think they get out much. Support Erin

Rae, a huge star back in Nashville had launched into her set without introduction and reeled off three songs. At the end of the third a voice at the front shouted, "Who are you?" not in a jovial fashion but in the manner of if you had found someone in your shed at 3am. She said horrified "Erin Rae. Who are you?" Despite all, Erin was brilliant. HGM's opening tune was off the excellent 2016 album 'Heart like a Levee' and was accompanied by a Lancashire voice reading out the full album review off his phone to the wife. Listen to the music! I was beginning to side with the man from Derby.

Just the two HGM members tonight, founder and ever-present Mike (MC) Taylor and his old mucker Phil Cook. Delightfully hirsute dishevelled look, like two lads returning through customs after a week in Amsterdam. Clearly great mates, this gig is just one happy haphazard jam. Bowie was a huge fan and described them as playing 'mystical country'. Mike tried to get mystical with a bit of philosophy "I've never been afraid of darkness, it's just a different kind of light" He looked up nervously to see how that one had gone down, and it had sailed many kilometres above the crowd's heads.

They know this part of the country well. When HGM first started, Mike trialled his music with Rick Tomlinson. That's the Bury folkie and poet and not the one of the Royle's couch. Mike is a huge fan of Ted Hughes and has spent time writing music in Todmorden. His love of poetry started at an early age reading shock kids verse." Shell Silverstein? Is he a thing over here?" Deafening silence, then one quiet voice "No"

Mike and Phil mused over the previous night's gig. Mike "It's great to do gigs in the north of England" Phil "Wow. Leeds" "Yeah, on the Sunday before a Bank Holiday" "There were some sights. Our hotel was a bit like a Salvation Army hostel this morning" They even now reside in a town called Durham in North Carolina which they described eyebrows raised as "An adorable recreation of the one in the north east of England" Both have wives and kids back home in the States but describe the urge to tour their music as irresistible. Mike tells the story of how he felt compelled to write a song for his first born which he now proudly plays at each gig. Since then he has been hit with the problem his youngest is now old enough to understand this and wants to know where her song is. Mike put heart and soul into penning a new song for her and excitedly gave her the first listen. Hands on hips totally non- plussed "That's fine" and walked off. Re-write required. They might well stop at two kids.

Great upbeat but bittersweet entertainment.

Top Tune: "Biloxi "Hiss Golden Messenger

Other Amateur Philosophers

Though a United fan, this was the night of the vaguely hilarious Mufc 0v3 Spurs. The worm has most definitely turned. Alex Ferguson used to beat Spurs with the team talk "It's Tottenham lads" Jose Mourinho chose to defend the result by asking the Press to consider his work as a whole entity and quoted the German philosopher Hegel." The true is the whole" He would do well to remember the philosopher and deep thinker at Old Trafford is always to be found in the number 7 shirt. Eric 'When the seagulls" Cantona is perhaps the most famed but there was also Michael Owen "It's hit the facial part of his head" and dear old Becks "We're definitely going to get Brooklyn christened but we don't know into which religion yet" and on time travel "That was in the past, we're in the future now"

Hollie Cook

After a night of torrential rain, think the health and safety officer had floated off. Work was flooded but the official advice was 'Just get on with it' Twelve hours of sodden misery. Only music and hot n sour soup could help.

Finally escaping the drudgery on the 192 bus, it became clear it caters exclusively for people escaping a recently committed crime. Central Manchester definitely has its own microclimate, the heavy rain replaced by a vicious horizontal snowstorm, blowing directly down Portland Street. Even the homeless were being driven off the streets, finding shelter wherever they could. I veered off onto Faulkner St and the Happy Seasons was for once only part full. I did well to get a table though, rocking the lost soul look. Pre drenched from the knees down after 12 hours without waders, and now covered from the knees up in a fresh layer of snow. My dining companions were two large Chinese family units who judging by the looks were totally oblivious to the blizzard. Sunday seems to be the day for the Chinese community, all immaculately dressed, though that wouldn't last long when they stepped out into that. They were sharing those huge mystery pots, I stuck with hot n sour and chilli beef. Great warming food and the world seemed better with a Tiger.

Double checked the listings. Had Hollie Cook beaten the elements to Gorilla? She is the daughter of Sex Pistols drummer Paul and is a one-time member of The Slits. Great heritage. Walking under the arch to Gorilla's ticket desk, the Eastern European looking bouncer approached with arm held up "Dude" he clearly thought looking at my dishevelled state I was one of the fleeing homeless "Can I pay in?" "Oh yeah sure. Sorry" Reggae on a Sunday night in a Manchester blizzard. Nobody is going to turn up, this will be a chilled night, can get right to the front. Pulled open that door and it was heaving, and a great night was had by all.

Hollie's voice is so cut-glass she could gate-crash a royal wedding. The huge crowd was buoyant, amiable, and equally as posh. Who knew Jamaican music was so Cheshire? For once I was glad of the heat in Gorilla. This was like being at a gig in Alaska. My favourite moment (but not of the three glamorous ladies next to me) was when Hollie reminded everyone it was Valentines this week. "So, a special hello to all you lovers out there. And if you are here on your own tonight, turn to someone next to you and give them a hug. The ladies shifted uncomfortably in their boots, I squelched awkwardly in mine. Great night.

Top Tune "Stay Alive "Hollie Cook

Home

Theatre was originally introduced to bring entertainment to the masses. One of the great misconceptions of the working class is that a night at the theatre can't be as good as a night in front of the telly. For one you just can't have a kip whenever you want. In fact, in my experience power napping is almost expected of you and positively encouraged. As long as you are not dressed like Alistair Sim in A Christmas Carol, nightshirt, sleeping cap and candle. Bag a seat away from the stage and get your head down during the boring bits. Also be careful if you are prone to waking up shouting "What was that!?" It can seriously disturb the ambience.

Row L at Home Theatre is a good spot for a snooze. All the aficionados cram into the first few rows. Sneak a look behind, if there is space get yourself back there, and let it all hang out. This clearly happened at the production of a very Long Day's Journey into Night. I was already sat in pole position L1 and quite alone during the first act. After a comforting interval Ovaltine, an old boy came along and said "Are those seats empty? it's a bit claustrophobic down there" I don't know who nodded off first, him or me. When Eugene O'Neil wrote this 210-minute masterpiece in 1941, no way did he expect everybody to stay awake all the way through it. In fact, he probably thought his editor would chop a good couple of hours off. To sit there for the equivalent of seven episodes of Emmerdale is some achievement. HOME is fine, if no real comparison to its much-missed predecessor The Cornerhouse. It is also a moot point whether it is possible to enjoy anything after being charged £10 for a glass of red wine. That's 3 bottles where I come from. In the future if the barman asks, "Is Castello rip off de Rothschild ok?" I won't pretend I've heard of it and just say "No. The cheap one please" A great production but by the end everyone seemed a bit delirious if not sleep deprived. The cast seemed ecstatic at remembering all them lines, the audience overjoyed at surviving an attritional night (but happily without one Go Compare or Winston Wolf). An emotional standing ovation broke out. That omnipresent amateur critic was there in the doorway as we queued to get out. Huge sigh "Wow. Epic. It made you laugh. It made you cry" Has she ever seen 101 Dalmatians? Now that's what you call a tearjerker

Top star: Galway actress Brid ni Neachtain

Top Tune: "Home" Edward Sharp and the Magnetic Zeros

Internet Dating

Purely for research purposes and absolutely nothing to do with being sad and lonely decided to have a go at internet dating. Signing up for the most upmarket one I thought I will never know anyone on here and one of the first faces I saw was a girl from school. The agony of having to find enough interesting facts about yourself to compile a profile and then take a selfie where you didn't look like someone from The Hills have Eyes.

Some of my prospective partners had profiles that must have been written by an advertising agency or JK Rowling. Hundreds of words detailing every aspect of their lives where they end up sounding like a sassy Mother Therese. My favourite was the woman who went to enormous lengths to say it was not all about money and good looks but then finished off by saying she was looking for someone who was "reasonably successful at their career and had good teeth" What if Jurgen Klopp was also on this site? What chance would you stand?

I always remember the advice Wreckless Eric's mam gave him "There's only one girl in the world for you and she probably lives in Tahiti" Whatever happened to, never ever put your kids down and no she couldn't lend him the plane fare. I prefer to hang on to the hope that the world is infinite. This means that in some parallel universe I'm living in a maisonette in Crumpsall with Lucy Verasamy. She works three days a week in Boots and I'm full time with Dyno-Rod.

Back to the profiling and had to seek advice from the helpful hints page. Tell them something interesting and vaguely romantic about yourself like have you ever been on the Orient Express or travelled Route 66? My ambition is to do Route 666 travelling the full length of Wales from the northern to southern tip. If you were awaiting execution what meal would you order as a last request? (Spring roll. Pudding, chips, peas and gravy in a tray. A Topic chocolate bar and a double Jack Daniels and coke) How could that be of interest to them? They wouldn't have time to make it for you, and Deliveroo wouldn't. Surely it would be more interesting to tell them how you ended up on Death Row in the first place. This was hopeless.

After days of agonising and paranoia I finally did get a reply, a forensic analysis of everything I had put from a Bolton primary school teacher, but still this was hopeful. Exciting times. We exchanged 'witty' playful messages. By SMS you get the first few words of the message then can view the full text when you log on to the site on your laptop. I was having a really painful day at work when I received a text "I really don't think we…." Brilliant she really did have a sense of humour. Couldn't wait to get home and see what the rest of the message said. "should meet up" That was it apart from two exclamation marks!! Whatever happened to Fridays, Brahms and Liszt and that single shopper's night at Sainsburys. The man who sent the first ever telegram was more successful than this. Robinson Crusoe was positively inundated. I retired after 4 months hapless searching without even a cup of tea or spring roll and got a cat.

Top Tunes: "Someone I care about" Modern Lovers "Whole wide World" Wreckless Eric

Manc Albums (c)

(11) Salford dance "Sounds from Nowheresville" 2012
(12) Moston baggies "Chicken Rhythms" 1991
(13) Bella Union dream pop "Suicide Songs" 2016
(14) Peter's post punksters "Music for Pleasure" 1997
(15) Art pop "Get to heaven" 2015

Ist Ist

Although forever in the shadows of its mighty neighbour St John's Cathedral, St Philip's on Chapel St has a beauty all of its own and is a special venue to watch live music. Frighteningly the local rock fans all have a slight look of Mike Sweeney about them. Just how busy was that man in the 70s 80s and 90s? There is something hugely enjoyable about quaffing cider in church, maybe it's just the irreverence and you can always take a pew between bands. The only problem here is that the sight lines are always interrupted by that eagle lectern that becomes more menacing the more cider you drink. Was it picked up from a Nazi party car boot? As the night progresses everyone edges slightly left away from it. Sinister.

St Philip's was the first church in this area c1825, and the original cobbled street remains. British museum architect Robert Smirke used to turn his hand to churches now and again and this was one of his finest. The cost of the build back then was £16 800, which would equate to about a month's wages for Alexis Sanchez today. £1.8m

Tonight, two old Blackthorn Festival favourites are on show. Irrepressible Dear Caroline's fierce approach should take them far, that's if they don't spontaneously combust somewhere along the way. They have brought huge support and I'm sure many of the young women are there simply to marvel at singer Joe Prior's sensational quiff. After a fine set, adrenaline still pumping they throw themselves around the Green Room or side altar as it's officially known.

Hugely powerful Manc tunes from the Ists, Adam Houghton's vocals harking back to early Joy Division. That Transmission like microphone effect sounds awesome on the tunes but when introducing the songs, it can sound like you are on Platform 13. Energetic and uplifting gig.

In St Phil's own blurb, it says, "This area is now one of the most desirable in Manchester whereas it used to be one of the poorest in the country" Certainly it's evolving rapidly into a much grander place. Even the short walk from town can become confusing if you don't do it regularly. I walked from Blackfriars mainly to see if The Rovers Return, Black Lion and Salford Arms are still open. Happily, yes to all three. Then just after here, near some new apartments it all started to look a bit unfamiliar. I had the choice of who to ask out of three people coming toward me, a thinner taller version of Neil from The Young Ones, a woman coming at great pace with what sounded like an empty tartan shopping trolley, or a menacing looking dude. As a rough rule of thumb regarding direction asking, always ask the least likely. Menacing dude laughed and said with the look of David Moyes when offered the United job "You going to church?" "I need to mate but it's a gig" Two well-dressed couples leaving the Aparthotel also had that 'Where the hell are we moment?' but then spotted the bright lights of Spinningfields just yards away across Victoria Bridge.

On the way out after the gig, one chap was on his Google maps and had already bumped into two people on the cobbled street. George Bush had nothing on this lad he really couldn't walk and read. I walked toward the New Oxford and there he was again bumping into street furniture. He was looking for Salford Central, so I told him I knew it. That set him off like Desert Island Discs on steroids. Great praise for both tonight's bands but his real love was Slow Reader's Club. Even though he looked like a trainee sales assistant at Argos, when SRC announced a mini UK tour my new clumsy friend went out and bought a ticket, for each leg of the tour! What kind of hours do you have to work in Argos to afford that? Sadly, the Manchester gig clashed with a planned trip to London to see 'School of Rock' A music tourist.

There was no respite, crossing Trinity Way he must have decided I was too old to know SRC and said his mum had recently introduced him to the joys of Orchestral Manoeuvres in the Dark and he had already been to see them. They had played with the Liverpool Philharmonic and Andy McCluskey had introduced the gig with "We are just going to play our 13 most famous songs" A further memory came back to him then and his face dropped "I've also seen the Thompson Twins recently. They were rubbish"

How glad I was to see Salford Central. I really hope it was a short train journey for the rest of the passengers. Coming to a Slow Reader's Club gig somewhere near you soon. Barking mad.

Top Tune: "Emily" Ist Ist

Istanbul

A fascinating city. Landing on one side of this gigantic metropolis at the military airport, the astounding journey across town was worth the trip price alone. 15 million people live here that's 2900 per square kilometre. Imagine being a leaflet distributor.

The previous night Napoli fans had fought a raging battle with Besiktas fans and police. For our game with Fenerbahçe, the Istanbul constabulary were taking no chances and were absolutely weighed down with riot gear. As a plane of old codgers in black laboured past to the waiting coaches they looked horrified. Like teenagers watching Open All Hours. Deprived of a night's entertainment, the helmets, shields and batons were literally hurled back into their wagons.

In a city of wondrous sights, we all wanted to see the Spice Market and did manage a brief glimpse of the Blue Mosque but the Bosphorous bridge alone was enough to take your breath away.

One thing that struck you en route across town were the small packs of slightly sun stroked dogs ambling about by the sides of the road. Sadly, the advice was still to stay as close to Taksim Sq. as possible due to the threat of attack. Here in the square the dogs seemed even more contented. A Turkish workmate tells me that most office workers take two packed lunches in the morning. One for themselves and one for a stray hound.

The bars just off the square proved disappointing so we ventured further into the cooler back streets. Somewhere along the way we acquired a United fan from Middleton in a denim jacket. After a few Efes we needed something to eat and stopped at the end of one busy street. The owner of the nearest restaurant came running over with menus. We asked if we could get a beer with our food. Momentary head scratching then "Come" and he took us and our menus further into the back of beyond. We followed him up some stairs and into a tiny bar. This was run by a very trendy westernised couple. They served us beer and he took our orders and brought the food from 100m down the street. What service. Everyone we met in Istanbul was ultra-friendly and ultra-dependant on the tourist industry.

Not to be outdone this area had a gang of cats. The resident in this bar was a very young tall white one. My chicken kebab soon became just a kebab. My nephew J realising it was fast approaching match time kicked off a round of rakis. As we were leaving the lady owner said "In Turkey we usually have one raki before or after a meal, not three with it"

It was all too much for denim jacket and we never saw him again. The most vibrant of cities with lovely friendly people. Must return one day without the football or raki.

Apart from those mad Russians, hooliganism is very much a minority sport these days. This hasn't impacted on the fans of Feyenoord of Rotterdam, who are still perfecting their ambush and attack tactics. Feyenoord fans had recently sacked the city of Rome.

Tremendous 40-degree heat in Holland for this match, and United supporters were mostly corralled into a concreted beer garden near Rotterdam train station. The bus to the ground was hugely entertaining. At one time as we passed a golf course, some locals sprang out of a bunker to hurl bottles and bricks. Due to the heat they were shirtless and two of the most prominent had dyed blonde hair and jeans held up by chain type belts. Much hilarity it was like being attacked by a 1980's Take That.

Another intriguing place. The architecture in this city is amazing if you get the chance to look and are not being chased by an enraged Jason Orange.

The implication that United fans are a bit elderly is hurtful to many. A mate of mine and his friends had been upset after leaving a town centre bar the night before. A young local in a rolled-up balaclava stopped them as they left. He had his gang waiting down a side street. Eyeing up the United fans he said, "Haven't you got anyone younger?" Very chivalrous.

Japanese in Chinatown

If Guardian food critic Jay Rayner thinks Bundobust is the most unassuming restaurant door in Manchester he has obviously never wandered Faulkner St looking for the minimalist gem Yuzu. The building still looks exactly as it did from its time as a Victorian warehouse. They also have a cunning plan to deter all non Nippons especially those the size of Jay. The vertical strip blinds on the door are more suited to a car wash and are low enough and heavy enough to wipe out anyone of above Japanese average height. Kylie would get under but could be wiped out by the whiplash effect if she was behind Jay. Brim full tonight so the only available seat is smack in front of the sushi bar with a view of wooden panels. Now you know how the Guinea Pig feels staring at the hutch door all night.

What Yuzu does have is friendly waiting staff, ultra-fresh food and a genius chef. I had the prawn gyoza starter and surely there is non finer in the western world. A masterpiece. The main course was scallop don which came with lovely sweet rice, miso soup, green beans and some fierce wasabi. If you ever wondered where Jack Nicholson got that expression from in The Shining, he had just had wasabi for lunch.

I had no idea what to drink but the waitress cheerfully recommended the Asahi Black Lager. No matter how crisp and light a lager it was, your brain was still telling you "You are eating raw fish with stout' This is the kind of place where people can't help but share. Two Londoners to my right were enjoying a huge piece of salmon between them and to my left two young Japanese lads were feasting on jumbo prawns, chicken katsu and curry sauce. The katsu looked incredible. Who knew chicken in breadcrumbs could look that enticing? Certainly not that chef in Kiev.

When not suffering severe food envy lusting after other diner's dishes that wooden panel vista can concentrate your mind on your own glorious food. With chopstick skills still at drunken kerplunk level it was a hard but determined fight not to lose my gyoza. I simply speared it lance like and didn't drop any. A proud moment. It was Jazz Festival time and they were playing some great old skool classics. A brilliant time was had by all. Belting grub and atmosphere 5/5

Still the Trip Advisor zealots found fault including "Bit pokey" and that one that I believe was from Jeremy Hunt "Slightly odd to find a Japanese in Chinatown"

Tram tactician

Young woman on her phone explaining to her boyfriend why she was on the 11pm tram home after work on a Friday night "There was a huge queue in Peter's Square at 6 o'clock so I went to the pub" Short reply "No I'm just a bit tired. Would you come and meet at the end of the road? It's so dark there" Even shorter reply." You'd be able to tell if I was pissed" Grunt "Love you, bye, bye" Hung up, dropped phone on tram floor, got an apple out of her handbag (No Listerine) Job done.

Japanese in Piccadilly Gardens

Those safari park grills in the Serengeti with herds of wildebeest strolling by. The sight of Sydney Opera House across shimmering water or a glimpse of the Eiffel Tower. What a difference to a restaurant to have that special view. Shoryu Ramen has Piccadilly Gardens. Could be the only restaurant in the world where you pay extra not to have a window seat.

On the day I visited there was a wire fence running down the middle of the Gardens to try and protect new turf that the Council had laid on the hottest day of the year. It hadn't worked but did have a look of the Serengeti about it. Scorched earth. Still there were plenty of families sunbathing who had brought the kids along to take advantage of the spa facilities provided by the fountains. Wild spice dealers roamed the perimeter fence. A great northern vista.

Shoryu's food is fantastic. To curb the heat, I jumped straight in with a Kirin Nana frozen lager. Not sure of the quality of the beer, it was too cold to tell. I didn't realise you were supposed to let the head melt a bit before sipping it. The first gulp had the same effect as a visit to Leslie Ash's doctor.

Kimchi Seafood Tonkatsu was lovely. Not a seafood expert I asked the waitress "What are them green sheets?" Deadpan reply but with a smile that said have you've had too much sun fat lips? "That's seaweed. It is very nice. I love it" No sign of a knife and fork here you just get chopsticks and a big ladle. I tried to take a quick tutorial by watching a Japanese lady who was sat just outside my window. No chance. Eating sea food broth with ladle and chopsticks was hazardous. Apologies to my neighbours. Great healthy tasting fresh food and a voucher that gives you your 10th Ramen free. Think they may have moved to a greener pasture by then. Brilliant lunch agonising view.

Jazz Festival

One thing Manchester really does embrace is a good old-fashioned festival. The Jazz Festival is now 23 years old and in 2018 comprised a total of 96 gigs. A diverse line up had attracted people from all over the world, well mostly it seemed the USA and Japan. Festival staff this year had been hired from the Fringe Festival, the lunatic fringe festival.

At the ticket office one Japanese lady was striving to buy tickets for tonight's glitzy gig at the Midland Hotel. Patiently she politely inquired, picking her words carefully. On the other side of the counter, one ticket clerk was shouting "The sun's too bright I can't see the screen" and the other couldn't speak because he had a mouth full of Quavers. They fobbed our patient friend off with a "You have to book at least 48 hours in advance" and she took it all with good grace. I was shocked that they had my Mali Hayes ticket for later that evening at Night and Day sat there on the desk. I moved off to the main Albert Sq. bar. A barmaid was busily wiping the bar with kitchen towel and then hurled it in the general direction of the bin only for it to wrap around the neck of a fellow staff member. Japanese lady witnessed this as well. All this way for this, no jazz just slapstick.

Mali Hayes is a fantastic talent from an established Manchester musical family. Her grandparents were classical musicians. Dad is a singer and mum Yvonne Ellis is a bit of a legend. If you recognise Yvonne it may well be from her time as sound engineer at classic Manc venue The Gallery on Peter St. She is doing the mixing tonight; you can guarantee no sound problems.

Two Bristol references tonight. The classy support band, We are Leif, hail from there and Mali had her tea round the corner on Church St at a branch of the world class Bristol pie maker, Pieminster. Mali says "It's so hot in here. I've been in Pieminster. I can't move" They feed you so well in there you can feel anchored. A mistake many of us have made pre gig in the Northern Quarter.

The two lads dancing manically front of stage had definitely been somewhere else for tea. I stood stage left with the photographers far away from that dreaded Night and Day column. That meant I was treated to Mali's full pre gig warm up. Toss of the hair and take sandals off. That was it, she is one cool lady.

With the backing of Giles Peterson and many other jazz watchers comparing her to Jill Scott, Mali will surely go far. With that heritage she readily mixes genres of urban, soul, jazz, rnb to great effect. I bet mum approves of her daughter's philosophy "You shouldn't have to be tied down to one thing. Just be yourself and do what feels right for you"

Top Tunes: "This feeling" "Back to me" Mali Hayes "I've found you" We are Leif

Two days later I returned to Albert Sq. to sample some Somtam Street Thai Curry from the festival food stalls and to see harpist Esther Swift. I'd seen Esther many years previously playing at the tiny cafe Love Saves the Day near Piccadilly Station. Tonight's band and crowd are much bigger. We are in Salon Perdu Spiegeltent, the luxury festival hub. It looks like a circus tent from the outside but inside it's more like Mick Jagger's Glastonbury glamp. Beautiful wooden floors, comfortable intimate booths and stain glass windows! Tonight, Esther has brought along a team of her Uni friends. That means violin, viola, cello, trombone, piano, drums and four harps. Four Harps is more than anyone has ever drunk.

Steve Mead is a highly entertaining and slightly bonkers compere. Tonight's piece, Steve tells us is called The Light Gatherer, the winner of the Irwin Mitchell, Manchester Jazz Festival Commission. It is loosely based on adopted Mancunian, Carol Ann Duffy's poetry. He informs us it comes in seven parts and Esther has requested "Please no applause after each movement" It was only next day when I remembered where I had heard this request before. It was at my doctors on my 50th birthday MOT. One movement called Text really stood out. It bemoans how the use of social media has destroyed the art of conversation. Happily, we get a repeat of it as an encore. Those four harps really did cast a spell. Engrossing and hypnotic stuff. Steve bounded back on at the end to thank the crowd for the first full standing ovation of the festival. Well deserved it had been enthralling. Then he said, "If you all want to stay on there is a Q&A on women's lack of representation in the music industry" A clever way to empty a hall. I went off to look for another Harp. Top Tune: "Text" Esther Swift.

Mali Hayes

John Murry at The Castle

"I'd like to start with a tribute to the great city of Manchester" said John Murry in his Southern Gothic drawl. The crowd winced 'Oh no not another version of Don't look back in Anger' A hush fell then John accapellaed "Got a fist of pure emotion, got a head of shattered dreams. Gotta leave it, gotta leave it all behind...Now"

"What the f*ck is up with that guy? Is he a f**king sociopath?" At last Gary Barlow exposed as a crazed stalker.

For any other artist of his status you would think this had definitely been an agent booking error. "Do you want to play at The Castle?" "A castle? Hell yeah" Not so with John, his full-on passionate performances are ideally suited to these smaller intimate venues that he loves.

Addiction problems and personal tragedy have haunted John's 38 years but what hasn't killed him has certainly made him stronger. Some can see only darkness in his music but there is real hope and inspiration here. He is forcefully making the point; we are all going to die soon and that soon is sooner than we think. So, get on with it now.

John has decamped to the Irish spa town of Kilkenny (Smithwicks and Kilkenny ales) to escape his problems but he is mega excited to be in "Manchester, the largest city in Ireland" Then a moment of doubt "Hang on, or is that Liverpool? There's one place they shake your hand for saying that and one place they head butt you"

Steeped in British musical culture, references are made to John Peel and Bob Harris and also an enquiry as to where the famous 'Joy Division on a snowy bridge' photo was taken.

Earlier the fragile but wonderful Mazzy Staresque support Nadine Khouri had told us her and her guitar had been forced to stand all the way from London on a four-hour train journey. Another artist suffering for her art.

Fittingly a large proportion of the crowd are in some state, the state of mildly deranged. There is an uncomfortable drunken bromance between two huge bearded types and some totally tuneless backing from two alcohol fuelled fanatics. Based either side of the hall, one male, one female their discordant appreciation wouldn't have got them an invite to the rest of the tour. As the middle part of the crowd melted away to protect their ears, our duettists ended up close together like Mariah and Luther singing 'Endless Love'

Despite joking he needed to write more pop songs, the undoubted stand out was the bleak and stunning "Little Coloured Balloons" Brutally honest, powerful with flashes of genius. What a gig. The crowd left mesmerised and John didn't even give his new backing crew the chance to singalong to the usual cheery encore, Townes van Zandt's "Waiting around to Die"

A week later the tour finished in Scotland and John was asked about the high spots "Glasgow is great, there are not many places like it. Manchester as well. I don't know about Liverpool but yeah Manchester" You've got to love this guy.

Top Tune "Come five and twenty" John Murry

In October 2019 me and Ali had a great chat with John outside Band on the Wall. Fantastic entertainment with everything from Bannon to Ballinasloe being discussed. John told of a night out with Nick Cave, Mark E Smith and Shane Macgowan. That's one episode of Come Dine with Me that has never been aired. He told us he is now learning Irish and has been totally adopted by his new homeland. People love to take him to the local rural disco, and he spoke of the first time he encountered the strange phenomenon of an Irishman on the dancefloor. Expression of fear, confusion and mild panic trapped in a body that wants to dance but just can't.

Keith's gone missing

In 2005 the Manchester Evening News declared that Oli Bayston and his band Keith were going to be "a force to be reckoned with for years to come". Q magazine said they would soon share Elbow's pedestal. Many others agreed. The debut EP was surely the most blissed out ever. A year later the four lads from Manchester University shared the partly prestigious, The Road to V Festival competition title with Bombay Bicycle Club who went on to fame and fortune. Keith on the other hand disappeared into the black hole that sadly can capture so much musical talent.

Not even musical differences i.e. mass brawl on the tour bus were cited as a reason. The journey to the top can be a mad game of snakes and ladders. Luck will always play a part. Being in the right place at the right time, mentally or physically can define musical history. What if the light hadn't been on when Paul Young (Sad Cafe) walked past? If the girl in the Freshies song had got a job in Greggs? The Nosebleeds might well have got into music school. MC Tunes might have named himself after a different throat lozenge. If Mrs Gallagher had settled in Hale, her sons might have written songs about tofu and not cigarettes and alcohol.

Fame can be hard to find and then flimsy and fleeting. Overnight sensations have almost always been grafting for years. Take care Pale Waves and Slow Readers Club.

After years working in the studio with the likes of Liane le Havas, Hot Chip and Bat for Lashes, Oli is now back with his own project, Boxed In. Championed by 6 Music they have an impressive following. Oli himself still looks younger than the paperboy. He is amazed by the full house at the Deaf Institute and astounded the young crowd are aware of his earlier work. In his dozen or so years in the studio he hasn't been too impressed by a lot of music that has passed him by. He was once asked 'What is the worst punishment the devil could devise?' He replied 'Listening to The Killers for eternity'

Top Tunes: Keith "Mona Lisa's Child "Boxed In "Forget "

Kunstmuseum

Gloriously United are drawn in Switzerland again so another chance to visit my great friend Svanette in Dornach near Basel. More vegan delicacies, a must return to the Goetheanum, and a couple of things I'd missed out on last time. The water taxi across the Rhine and a visit to the world-famous art gallery Basel Kunstmuseum.

On the morning of my flight I had been to Moose on Fountain St for a Double Dutch breakfast. Two pancakes, one with bacon, one with sausage meat, sprinkled with maple syrup and two fried eggs perched happily on top. The seriously slim waiter said unconvincingly "Yes! That's my favourite too. I always have that" which is not what Little Swan would have said.

My first Swiss breakfast consisted off an Alpine grass and apple smoothie with some edible flower heads, buckwheat, almonds, plums and black tea. That's what you call a breakfast Mr Moose waiter. Couldn't resist a few trips back and forth across the Rhine in the waxi, till the girl doing the steering "Oh you are back again" was sick of me. At less than £3 a go, quite simply the best and cheapest thing to do in Basel.

The Kunstmuseum is spectacular and needs to be good to compete. These people know their art. It was here in 1661 that the first art collection in Europe was thrown open to the public. Now the city of Basel has over 40 museums!

Brilliant world-weary security man on the door. His experience spotted a greenhorn straight away. "Do you have a ticket?" "No" "Out the gate 50m on your right" When I got back, "You can't bring that bag in, you have to put it in the locker" His expression screamed like a Munch "What are you even doing here?" Good question.

Some big hitters work on show. Picasso, Chagall, Dali, Magritte. All wonderful stuff but to a seriously untrained eye my favourite was by Maria Helena Vieira da Silva. Definitely would have bought that one. If it had been the 6th form art project and I was the teacher I would have said "You know Maria you could just make a living out of this" and to Fernand Leger "Listen mate there's still time to get on the General Studies course"

The game against the Young Boys was in the Swiss capital, Berne. Thankfully the club had seen sense some time ago and changed the name of their stadium from the Wankdorf to the Stade de Suisse, which saved a lot of embarrassment for Cockney Reds asking for directions.

It was well over 30 degrees on the day of the match, way too hot for sightseeing. No option but to seek some shade in Adriano's bar. Inspirational krautrock was playing "There's no time to waste, we are the human race" As I was paying up the cheerful and mildly impressed barman said, "I can't remember how many you have had?" You can't! It's either 6,7 or 8"" Let's call it 6. 30

CHF" Deal. They were only large halves, but the average Swiss would call 2 a sesh.

I moved on to the bar opposite the Parliament buildings in the Old Town. Security seems quite relaxed here. Most of the locals moved when one gang came in. The barmaid told me that once every three months, the Mayor, local MP's, and Council leaders come in and have a sing song to show they are one with the people. The people respond by all going to sit outside. The politicos burst into a mind-blowing Y Viva Espana which had me wondering just which flower heads I'd consumed. If Carney and Stringer tried this there would be serious civil unrest.

The match wasn't that exciting until the heavy-handed riot police objected to about 100 or so of us leaving early for our train back to Basel. Much banging of shields and sabre rattling. The situation seemed to be deteriorating. One female officer walked over and sorted it within seconds. Women eh? Saw my old mate Ste and his gang on the train back. As the train hurtled through Swiss countryside, they were discussing just who was best, cats or dogs. They really have been travelling together too long.

Next morning, I said my goodbyes to the Little Swan and headed off to spend my last francs in town. Another wonderful stay in Dornach. Back across that Rhine on the water taxi. She definitely was sick to death of me now. Headed into the first restaurant I saw, The Schlosselzunft. It was a real classy joint and the waitress was absolutely stunning. I struggled not to betray my out of depthness but then pure panic set in when I needed a wee. I said to her in a Prince Charles accent "Excuse me, where is the bathroom?" With an over exaggerated perplexed look she replied, "The bedroom?" Was still red faced when I was paying the bill. Great trip. Top relaxed city. Lovely people.

La Luz

Who would have thought the two coolest bands in the world right now, La Luz and Khruangbin both sound a little like The Shadows? Hank Marvin could make a fortune guesting with both bands if he wasn't nearly 80. La Luz have a great mash up of Tex-Mex, 60's soul, Hank, surf rock, dream pop, bossa nova, Motown and more Hank. My friend Ali says if she could be in one band it would have to be La Luz.

Fittingly for the dreamy nature of many of the tunes, singer Shana reveals many of the songs come to her in her sleep. Maybe some in nightmares as there is hidden darkness in some of these lyrics. She looked a little aggrieved when her attempted compliment "I love Manchester it's so like California" prompted only hysterical laughter and an audible "Nooo!!!" Maybe she was thinking of her hometown of Seattle where she says 'The weather is always shitty'

Part way through Shana somehow parts the packed crowd for a dance off to 'Damp Face'. This brings looks of horror to the faces of the super cool Soup Kitcheners 'She wants us to do what?' Thankfully there was one exhibitionist who braved the potential scorn. Luckily keyboard player Alice jumped down and saved the day with some slick moves.

An absolute joy of a gig. Who knew that synchronised, reverb heavy line dancing could look so erotic? Blissful stuff and still hopelessly in love with drummer Marian. Catch them when they return you won't regret it. 5/5

Top Tunes: "Brainwash" "Cicada" La Luz

Khruangbin

These are truly an amazing band combining familiar genres like psych, soul, funk and Hank in a truly original way. The chemistry between all three band members, Mark, Laura Lee and Donald is astounding. Really never seen anything like it before.

I had hopped down to the Albert Hall on one leg with only my dodgy Achilles for company. Dismay the queue to get in stretched right up the road and even turned left towards the town hall. The touts were patrolling the most expectant queue I've ever seen. Almost religious fervour. I had a spare but didn't want it to go to them. After pogoing about for a bit thinking I won't be able to stand on this for more than an hour or so. I retired to the Abercrombie to think it over. I hopped off down the side street near Rev de Cuba and bumped into a couple I'd seen earlier who'd had the same 'swift half will half the queue' thought. She was impressed by my indie hopping. I told her it was a new injury and I hadn't worked out how to limp yet. "Oh, then when you get in, tell them you are injured, and they might let you in the VIP bit"

After a couple of pints, the queue had all but gone and the Long John Silver impression came easier. Sold my spare to a lad outside Rudy's who was so elated he looked like he'd got the keys to heaven. Told them I was struggling with injury at the venue door "Wait by that radiator someone will come and get you" A lad came and escorted me to a roped off area just above and to the band's left. He looked me up and down with "Yep nothing wrong with you" written all over his face until I accidentally booted some woman's handbag on the journey. She looked at me with "What did you do that for Hoppy?" Finally, there behind the red rope, a sensational view of the action and waitress service. Glorious.

From this vantage point you could see just how beguiled the crowd were. A sea of wonderment. Only brief anecdotes from the band. Guitarist Mark was so impressed and said sincerely "Thank you so much for singing along to a load of songs without words" The mesmerising Laura Lee recounted how on their first visit to Manchester they'd tried to be down with the kids and use some local slang on stage. In the heat of the moment she had got her fit, thick and sicks mixed up and actually signed off with "Thank you so much, you are thick as fuck"

Supreme night out. Looking out on that sea of smiling faces you can see how bands get hooked on performing for life. Gig of the year, by a mile. 5/5 Hopped home happy.

Top Tunes: "People Everywhere (Still Alive) ""White Gloves" "Maria Tambien "Khruangbin

La Luz

Khruangbin

Langworthy: Taste of Portugal

Another suburban restaurant definitely worth a visit is Taste of Portugal in the boutique village of Langworthy. Those upside-down houses on the Chimney Pot estate have always appealed, simply as you don't have to make it up the stairs after a night out. United were due to meet Benfica in Lisbon in a week's time so I thought I would get my eye in regarding the Superbock. Only three of us in on a midweek afternoon. One was having a fine-looking pork stew and the other the Portuguese national dish Bacalhau, salted cod (of all the great dishes, why??) I settled for some prawn dishes with lashings of Superbock and Piri Piri sauce.

I had asked the waiter about the district I was going to stay in, but he was too Portuguese to understand. Instead the salted cod lad answered. Andy was half Lisbon and half Horwich and had been home for couple of days for his countries World Cup match against the Swiss. To Portugal not Bolton.

He had promised his daughter the Portuguese delicacy of a chocolate salami as a present but had forgotten it. He was just about to buy it at the airport when his son spotted young midfielder Renato Sanches. After a few selfies the salami slipped his mind again. So now he had made the shorter journey knowing Taste of Portugal stocked it in their shop. Salford Salami. A wise man. As a parting tip he said "Stay off the ginja in Lisbon"
Sadly, I didn't which led to a painful 4 am encounter with some local reprobates. As I detailed to police, one looked like a geriatric version of the lead singer of Aswad with two grey dreadlocks. One was dressed in a maroon puffer jacket, had a tiny head and was only the size of Willie Carson and another looked like Boris Johnson with a permatan. What an identity parade that would have been. To be honest Willie Carson would have been enough. Wrong time wrong place.

Lisbon is a great town. Euro aways are usually a total delight with the only down point being 90 minutes of drab football. A great chance to visit the best cities in Europe.

Amazingly months later I got an e-mail in Portuguese from a Lisbon police station. A lad at work translated "We have your phone; can you come and pick it up"

Lily from Ashton

Had always wanted to visit Lily's veggie cafe in far, far away Ashton under Lyne. It was only uncertainty over the visa arrangements needed for travel that had stopped me. For someone from close to the airport this is the other side of the world. The very end of the wagon trail or metro system. Finally, after seeing yet another 5* Lily's review, probably from Thom Hetherington, just couldn't resist any longer. Correct decision, what a joy it is. Even though the cafe is right next to the tram stop, I still managed to miss it, as it is near hidden by a car park hedge. What a mix of languages and accents round here. Somehow the Gujarati Tameside was easier to understand than the Trad Tameside. The youngsters staple "Do you know what I mean?" which is slow and extravagantly drawn out in Wythenshawe is completely different down here, short and staccato. "Jowotamin?" "No"
This was in the burning heat of June and it quickly became clear that clothing for both male and female is optional down here if the temperature tops 60 degrees. Some fearful frazzled sights. Burnt strap lines or pink beer bellies or both. Give them roller skates this could have been a dystopian LA boardwalk.
Anyway, soon found the cafe and the food and ambience were superb. Papdi chaat, paneer toofani with roti and even took a vegetable Kolhapur take away for my sister. I still managed to miss a trick. Back in work a few days later an Indian colleague was dismayed I hadn't sampled one of the orange flavoured sweets. "The best you'll find in Manchester"
Let's hope they keep the informal American diner look and atmosphere when they make their long-promised move across the road into new premises. 5/5
Do you know what I mean and other new language
The only one I can handle is peng. Oh, for a remake of Breakfast at Tiffany's where the George Peppard character says to Holly Golightly "Yo Holly is anyone ever tell you right, you is peng" Thanks to the Wythenshawe schoolkids from Brookway (Institute of Health) for that direct quote. I wonder if that romance will last. I was on a tram once passing Brookway when the building work was being done. An old couple in front were looking out the window chatting away. Her "They are making that place into an

111

Academy you know?" Him "Why because it's rubbish?" Her "Yeah"

In Chorlton they definitely have a whole different vocabulary. A young trendy dad with his son got on the metro. The youngster was taking videos and his father said to him "I hope you've got the appropriate attribution for that" I've no idea.

Thankfully back over the motorway in Northern Moor came a more familiar conversation. The Wythenshawe good parenting manual was out. A young mum in her mid-teens with her little one being advised by two experienced old heads in their late teens. Looking to the future "Always, always have that 3-year gap, every time" Then on a shared friend "Is Bec still with that Callum?" "Ugh he's a bit of a freak" "Yeah he only eats baked beans" "The liar I saw him in Nando's last week" Could have listened to them all day and sadly didn't get to hear the full story of baby Lundin. Another child named after where it was conceived. Vicar "How are you spelling that again?"

Looking for Laura; life is much stranger than fiction

At the Wargirl concert, the person having the most fun tonight was stood just in front. She was with a friend who wasn't quite feeling it as much. He only had half a pint, then left it on the shelf next to me and departed mid gig. She just shrugged and carried on drinking and dancing regardless. At the end both of us chatted to singer Samantha Parks and thanked her for such a mind-blowing performance. Sam was overjoyed with that, thanked us and made her way off, leaving just us two fans in the venue. I said, "Are you having a pint?" and off we went on a mad journey. No drugs were abused along the way!

I told her she must try an Old Fashioned in the Terrace bar and she didn't flinch. Like moths to a light, everyone seemed drawn to her. Conversations broke out everywhere. One bloke spotting the Stringfellow like age difference asked, "Where did you two meet?" "Downstairs about two minutes ago"

She had been to Uni a few years ago so I asked if she had put the degree to good use. Straight faced and without hesitating she replied "No not really I'm in the sex industry" I would have bet the house on her saying primary school teacher. I nearly choked on the orange peel. This just didn't ring true. Laura (Not her real name. Her real name was Madame XXX) said she wasn't at the coal face but was more of a booker for a hooker. Still shaking my head, she produced her phone and showed me a list of messages, all very polite, requesting some very impolite things. I think tellingly they were all spelt correctly, well I think that's how you spell it. Who knew this industry was so niche?

We had a great chat and she ended up giving me relationship advice. Yes was closing so we walked back toward town. Opposite The Garratt she decided she really needed a wee. There was a lad stood outside Spar smoking something herbal. She marched straight up "Do you live here? Could you let me in to use the toilet?" She was certainly direct. I was expecting a two-word response. He had shorts on and fetchingly a thick pair of grey socks under his flip flops and had the look of Viraj Mendes. He said he lived in a flat above the Spar with his sister and would let my charming new friend in for a wee. Surreal. Would love to say I couldn't believe any of this but by now I was in the zone. The twilight zone. Disaster struck, he searched for the key and couldn't find it. Rang his sister and there was no answer.

The three of us went into 5th Avenue. I looked like grandad out with his innocent looking grand-daughter (who by now was literally hopping) and a Sri Lankan asylum seeker. She hurried straight to the loo, then we had a shot at the bar which she promptly threw up. Madame X and Viraj (him in his flip flops) had a dance to some headbanging rock and we left to the bemusement of the door staff. Thought you had saw it all before did you?

Viraj got a phone call from his worried sister, who in fact was really his cousin and they were from the Maldives and he invited us in to meet her. These Maldivians are trusting folk! In time honoured fashion I couldn't get my shoes off at the door as requested but we sat chatting till 2am then me and X set off looking for her bike! She could locate it on her phone but not in reality. Exhausting. I left her to it. She had put her name and number in my phone. As I went on my bewildered way she shouted "If you are going to Neighbourhood Festival ring me" My mate D, the wise old sage of Chorltonville just wouldn't believe this story at all. So, I turned hopeless Colombo. Amazingly she had put her real name in my phone but only 10 digits of the number. A quick google and there she was, a poet and short film maker. A genuine head the ball or great actress. Oh well stardom beckons. Where are my royalties? I miss her.

Lyon: Two trips one planned

Just before a trip to Lyon a gang of us had celebrated a mate's 50th birthday in Blackpool. High spirits (top shelf), some irresponsibly placed street furniture (must write to the council) and a cobbled street left me with a bang on the head that would have put Ziggy Stardust to shame. Amazingly I was picked up and sponged off (not a euphemism) by a passing lady of the night. It's funny how like wounded animals, humans show more empathy towards injured comrades. Sat near a Manchester Airport bar less than 48 hours later I was joined by an old boy from Glossop "Ouch! Oh, don't worry. Last year I had a blackout crossing the road and knocked my front two teeth out. £350" and he showed off his gleaming new gnashers.

On the way home waiting for the connection in Southampton Airport I sat at the same cafe table as a Northern Irish woman who fantastically had the full-on Jim McDonald accent, so she did. She recounted the story of her and a friend travelling to Tenerife for a week's holiday. Her mate fell out of a taxi on the first night and she had fallen trying to pick her up, blacking both eyes. They spent the next six days indoors and returned to a universal "You didn't get much of a tan"

Every time you hear that accent you wonder if The Kursaal Flyers smash would have been a hit if they had been from Armagh "Little does she know...so she doesn't. That I know that she knows...so I do. That I know she's two timing me...so she is"

Have been lucky to visit Lyon before and one of the first things you see is the wonderful roof over the Rhone-Express station, like an eagle in flight. Stunning. Lyon is a culinary capital but last time we had been in search of a Chinese and mistakenly thought the correct name for one was 'Chino' not 'Chinois' Greeted at the doors of some of the finest restaurants in Europe we were shouting back at them "Trousers? Trousers?"

Language and food were to crop up many times on this trip too. Having found the general area I was staying in; I asked a very fast-moving local lady if she knew Rue Bardeau. Hair swept back, grey sweatshirt, no make-up and very rapid in her pink trainers but oh so chic. Without breaking stride, she answered, "Ah I live very near here but I'm not so sure" On she sped and recruited two other very helpful ladies and we stormed on like a migrating herd. In Manchester we don't walk this fast.

At the bottom of a huge set of concrete steps "Oh your apartment is just up there on the left" and off all three charged. This is a fast moving city.

The directions were perfect. This was where the old silk workers of Lyon were once housed. At the very top of the hill is Croix Rousse which has a bewildering market about the length of Deansgate. The stalls here on both sides of the road sell everything on earth including United bed linen. Anyone who thinks all French bars have classy names would be in for a shock. The local pub is called The Dog's Bollocks.

Lyon's magnificent amphitheatre was directly outside my apartment. Saint Blandine and other Christians were slaughtered right here by the Romans in June 177. In a bizarre twist, in the field next to it, two old foes were living side by side. Wild cats living alongside a pigeon coop. The looks they were giving each other.

I'm sure a Madchester documentary must have been shown in Lyon recently. Two ladies outside a cafe were having a very animated conversation and suddenly one of them started singing the praises of "Johnee Marr". At a pizza joint the young girl behind the counter asked where I was from "Yay Manchester is cool. Lyon people are not so cool, they are chilly urgh" and shuddered.

One night we ventured for a curry. The salad with the starter had beetroot and olives in it, and the naan bread was filled with cream cheese. Heaven before heart attack.

Lyon is situated at the conference of the Saone and Rhone rivers. All Roman roads led here, and it was the capital of Gaul. The Catholics massacred the Huguenots here in 1572 (Nigel Farage is a Huguenot) More recently in WW2 it was a stronghold of the French resistance.

One old boy who I'm sure was a descendant of the Resistance was the owner of the fantastically atmospheric Le Sathonay restaurant. When I said to him "Sorry my French is not good" He looked in mock horror "My English is not very good" then laughed, slapped me on the back and said "We will get by" He served up the finest steak, spuds and shallots you could imagine. Strangely you can't get a scrambled oeuf anywhere in Lyon. For breakfast found myself in a real young funky joint called Le Tigre. It was Fair-Trade, vegan and gluten free. A real indie haven with some great French jangly tunes playing. Trying to be down with them enfants I asked the owner "Have you heard of Francois and the Atlas Mountains?" (They sound French) A very definite 'Non' Didn't realise they were from Bristol.

On the basis of Ziggy Stardust drawing too much police attention I gave my match ticket to my nephew and watched the game in Dams bar. After 3 days drinking in here, one of the staff finally pointed at the cut on my head. I said "Jack Daniels" and all the bar staff, and some customers nodded knowingly "Aah Jack Daniels"

Familiar sight on the way home. I was heading back through Southampton which was the cheaper option, Manchester was at the next desk and Newcastle next door to that. With delays all three were now scheduled to depart within minutes of each other hence chaotic queues. I let a very posh Winchester woman in front of me who had got caught in no man's land. She was very thankful but then noticed the Ziggy which had now morphed into two Harold Lloyd black eyes "Oh have you been skiing?" "No ballooning" "Really?" "No, no" "It must have been something dangerous" "Yep Jack Daniels"

Top Tune: "Grand Dereglement" Francois and the Atlas Mountains

Manchester Museum

The first thing you see on entering the museum is the skeleton of Maharajah, the huge elephant who used to draw the crowds at nearby Belle Vue Zoo. In 1872 Belle Vue owner John Jennison had purchased Maharajah in Edinburgh for £680. Really hope that was late at night in a pub and the next morning he opened his eyes slowly in the hotel room 'What have I done?'

In a masterstroke of publicity his keeper Lorenzo Lawrence walked Maharajah all the way down to Manchester, a journey of ten days and over two hundred miles. The story was that Maharajah was due to travel by train, but he had taken the carriage roof off with his huge tusks. Either that or the Northern Rail guard had said 'You're not coming on here with that'

Jennison was from Adswood and had a mildly successful aviary before building up the Belle Vue site from scratch. At first it was just 'a tearoom with four monkeys and a borrowed pelican' but grew to be a huge tourist attraction and the first privately funded zoo in England. In the early years you could buy an expensive season ticket for its gardens and many well-heeled people would arrive from Manchester to dance and listen to the genteel music. Unfortunately, the gardens had a side gate to Longsight, and it was reported "Roughs in coarse clothing were embarrassing middle class ladies by attempting to dance with them" This tradition passed on to Bredbury Hall.

Maharajah lived for a decade at Belle Vue, was hugely popular and did the celebrity circuit, taking part in many parades. Lorenzo was to stay on for over forty years. You always learn something new on each visit to the museum. Who knew that Arthur Brooke, an Ashton lad, set up the first Brooke Bond (PG Tips) shop at 23 Market St, Manchester in 1869? There never was a Bond, it was just Arthur's imaginary friend.

Some amazing scenes today as three teachers manage to keep 40 six-year olds quiet. It later transpired that one sentence had guaranteed the silence "Stan the T-Rex lives here, and he is watching"

I gained a love for rock and fossils from my sister H. Tremendous varieties on show here from near and far, Ammonites, Trilobites, Stockport Sandstone, Matlockite, Brazilian Rutile and even a fossilised Rochdale scorpion. To my knowledge scorpions only died out in Rochdale during the last century. Pele's Hair, thin strands of volcanic glass, is my favourite exhibit. Lava ejected from volcanoes, cooled and stretched by the wind then blown a distance away. In Manchester City's museum they have some Franny's Hair, an entirely different thing. Months later I took H to see the specimens and due to refurbishment, they had been moved into storage. Mothballed fossils. They will return in 2021, when we all be more fossilised.

Still there is so much more to see and if you want an honest review it's always wise to check out the kids post it note message board.

"It is amazing here because I found out humans used to look like apes" "Liked looking at Egyptian history but really love the frogs" "Many of us have Neanderthal DNA" and the overall winner "I need a poo"

Mackie Mayor

Mackie Mayor is Manchester's sparkly food hall on Eagle St, in a long-neglected part of the Northern Quarter. The building is one of two that survive from the days of The Smithfield Meat Market. The other is home to the excellent but woefully under publicised Manchester Craft and Designer Centre. Mackie was completed in 1858 the building named after the standing Manchester mayor, Ivie Mackie. You can bet the present incumbent Bandwagon Burnham would love something to still be bearing his name in 160 years' time. Maybe Burnham Spice Gardens, a circular cycle route of the city centre or even HSB, High Speed Burnham.

As a working building it had closed in 1972 and fell into disrepair. Grade 2 listed it has survived many dubious incarnations since including time as a skate park. When empty its relatively isolated location made it popular with the homeless and some of the pithier and cleaner graffiti from these days has been retained. The other brickwork spruced up and left bare and that amazing glass roof restored to its pristine glory. The shiny gym floor was not long ago bounced by Manc schoolkids. It's a spectacular place. Price wise it's been modelled on Lisbon's Time

Out, atmosphere wise on its smaller sister in Altrincham, and beard wise on Kabul market.

That glass roof can act as a greenhouse in summer, so another old school reference comes in handy. The canteen like wooden tables are lined with cloudy plastic jugs of water. Real drinks come from Reserve Wines and Spirits and local ales from Blackjack bar. I went first week in August and there was a large majority of teachers having a well-earned six weeks rest. The Aperol Spritz seemed to unleash a full year's emotion from one and bizarrely her friends just let her cry it out. Must be in the training manual. Mackie is also, child, dog and veggie friendly and you are never far from one or all of them panting and complaining of hunger. Having paid £11 for my pea and ricotta pizza, nothing was going to stop me from enjoying it. £11 for peas, dough and leaves, surely that can't be worth the outlay. It was outrageously good but do the Education Department know teachers can afford this sort of thing. To call it street food is a bit steep unless you live on the kind of street Michael Gove lives on.

It was too hot to move very far so wedged myself into the corner of Reserve bar and attempted to navigate through the Gin menu with a couple of unscheduled stops for a Limoncello (curiosity, someone else had ordered one) and a sangria. The barmaid told me she had freshly made it. Three bottles of Merlot, a bottle of Triple Sec, a couple of limes thrown in and a hint of lemonade. Great jug. Powerful.

The first barman was well impressed I clocked his accent as being from Stalybridge and he told me the term Staleyvegas had been coined by his neighbour (Think he thought I'd had the full sangria jug). He assured me things were changing out there, with plush new apartments going up and it isn't just known now for "The train station bar and violence"

His shift replacement had an in-depth knowledge of all thing's alcohol. He could predict an order simply by watching the customer's walk to the bar. At least that was true until the blubbing woman rocked up. I shocked the barmaid by identifying the sound systems "Fade into you" after two notes. Ginned up to the gills I told her Hope Sandoval was the most beautiful woman ever in rock music. She had never heard of her but was able to Google her on the till. "Wow she really is"

Space-age till, biodegradable straws but still the contactless card reader wouldn't work. Must have overheated. Wise beyond her years, the barmaid's raised eyebrows, when I decided (ordering a fifth gin) that the thing I needed most in the world was a bottle of Saki to take home, told me it was time to make tracks. Ace place to go, cool despite the heat. Well worth the journey if you are craving gin and dough.

Top Tune: "Fade into you" Mazzy Star

Manchester Mummy

These days the Manchester mummy is most likely to be spotted shopping at Asda or doing the school run in pink pyjamas and slippers but for years we had our own take on the Egyptian version.

Hannah Beswick was a wealthy Oldham woman in the 1700s who had inherited the grand Cheetwood Old Hall where she had been born in 1688. One of the greatest terrors of the 17th,18th and 19th centuries was the fear of being buried alive. Known as Taphophobia the macabre theme featured heavily in much of Edgar Allan Poe's work. Tales abounded of exhumed coffins with deep scratch marks from bloodied fingers as the victim desperately tried to escape from an early entombment. This led to Safety Coffins being patented with escape mechanisms and the setting up of the jolly Association for the Prevention of Premature Burial (meet every Friday the 13th, Church Hall)

Hannah's family had a real close shave with the phenomenon. Her brother John had been found in a catatonic state. Did they have the same breweries in Oldham back then? Popular opinion pronounced John dead. One relative though noticed that John's eyes were flickering just as they were nailing the coffin lid down. Up stepped Beswick family doctor and local celeb Charles White and declared John very much alive. He went on to live a long and happy life but the memory never quite left Hannah. (Many years later the day after the 1999 European Cup Final we discovered placing a mirror under the patient's nose is an easy way of checking for breathing and despite the complete lack of signs of life, Gilbo was still with us)

Doctor White himself was a fan of the macabre and like many of the medical profession of the time his deep fascination with death led him to keep a house full of oddities. This included the skeleton of the Gentleman Thief, Highwayman Higgins of Knutsford. Not knowing he was a nutcase, in her will Hannah instructed Doctor White that on her apparent death her body was to be kept above ground and given an occasional medical just in case. The case he used was that of an old grandfather clock at his home in Sale. Despite being paid handsomely he went against Hannah's wishes. In his professional opinion she did die without reasonable doubt in 1758. So, using the most up to date methods of the time he set out to embalm poor Hannah. The process involved filling the veins with a mixture of turps and vermillion,

removing all the organs before shrinking them and putting them back, squeezing out all the body fluids and sealing all cavities with plaster of Paris. The very earliest form of Imodium..
Thereafter she became the centrepiece of the good doctor's dinner parties. Her shrunken face peering out from the old clock case. The things that go on behind closed doors in Sale.
Eventually the 'Manchester Mummy' was gifted to the forerunner of Manchester University, Owens College to satiate the public's love and curiosity of all things Egyptian. It became the most popular exhibit ever. Finally, 110 years after her death the professors saw sense, decided she was most definitely not coming back and poor Hannah was finally and quietly laid to rest in Harpurhey Cemetery. Even this wasn't without problems as Dr White had never issued a death certificate so Madame Beswick's final resting place is in an unmarked grave. Not surprisingly an exasperated Hannah upset by her treatment from all and sundry returned to haunt the floors of Ferranti, Hollinwood the factory built on the site of the old family home. You can't blame her.

Glaspy and Vollebeck

If Margaret Glaspy ever went on 'Who do you think you are?' I'm sure she would discover her roots are in Ulster. When her great grandparents arrived on Ellis Island "What surname is it?" "Gillespie" "Sorry who?" "Gillespie" "Thank you Mr and Mrs Glaspy"
Tonight, her tour takes her to Deaf Institute supported by someone who thankfully missed Ellis Island and landed in Canada, Leif Vollebeck. Leif hits us with some very funny Canadian anti-American jibes. He saves his compliments for our city "Manchester is just the coolest place" and then one that could only be uttered by someone who has never lived here "Wow that rain is so moody" He even manages a 20 second history of the 7 years' war and asked if anyone had heard of General Wolfe. Shoegazing for me but thankfully a few had, including the solitary couple perched up on the balcony. Leif hadn't even noticed the balcony "Hey look at you up there! You look like The Muppets" Back to business and as he re-tuned for the next song,

he said, "Thank you for giving us our country" There was no French dissension.

He dedicated the fantastic 'Elegy' to one of his heroes Prince. On the day he first recorded the song, someone gave him tickets to see Prince play one of his last ever gigs. Fittingly it is a haunting song. Leif also spoke with great enthusiasm about his last visit to Manchester when he supported another hero of his, Gregory Alan Isakov "Anyone heard of Greg?" Silence. Less than General Wolfe.

Margaret is disarmingly waif like, belying the intensity of that voice. Powerful songs with terrific lyrics that will break your heart but also have a great hook. No filling here, the whole album is just 34 minutes long. Margaret is a master of the 3-minute tune and live they are definitely at their best, without any heavy-handed production.

The tone of her guitar is gorgeous and perfectly suited to the Deaf Institute acoustics. Her boyfriend is world famous jazz guitarist Julian Lage and she had 'borrowed' it off him a while back. What great conversations they must have over the Rice Krispies about Telecasters.

Marge is in a serious mood tonight. This is an occasion she is determined to bare her soul and she works hard at doing so. Usually a midweek crowd at DI are as deep as an Atlantic trench but are these all impostors? There seems to be plenty of boho chicks, indie kids, and beards but when Margaret makes an impassioned plea for a better world "Love is the best option right?" nobody seems to be listening. There is not one single whoop or yeah.

A raised eyebrow from Marge. She had to do a take two. This time they are with her with a huge cheer. From now on there is a bond. Phew.

After Leif's tribute to Prince, Margaret song checks Neil Young, Paul Simon and Elliott Smith and there is a lovely totally stripped back version of Lauryn Hill's 'Ex Factor' A huge talent

Top tunes "Elegy" Leif Vollebeck "Somebody to Anybody" Margaret Glaspy

YouTube "No Matter Who (Behind the Glass Sessions) Margaret Glaspy

Mattiel; will be huge

Mattiel Brown has taken the unusual but often traditional path to stardom, her determination overcoming illness and shyness on her journey to the top. One of her first reviews complained she was a bit static on-stage, tonight that brown bob haircut is bouncing everywhere. Ferocious uninhibited dancing. What a mix of influences, very old school rock n roll, soul, funk, punk and rockabilly and even mid gig "Do we all like a little country and western?" Brought up an only child on an isolated farm by her mum near Atlanta, Georgia she was restricted to listening to her mother's 3 albums, The Monkees, Donovan, and Peter, Paul and Mary. She later fell in with the Atlanta musical InCrowd and has played with the brilliantly named Jonah Swilley, Travis Murphy, Jordan Manley and Randy Michael since. Jordan in particular is on fine form tonight and beats the living daylights out of that drumkit.

You could be excused for thinking that support act Honey Harper is also from Atlanta with a name like that, but his real name is Bill. Problems for Bill tonight as he and his band's glam-country introspective harmonies are all but drowned out by the chattering classes at the bar. Then with a masterstroke he finishes with an emotion drenched "You don't have to say you love me" and Dusty's hit earns him a huge ovation.

For Mattiel this could have been a come down from the weekend's career high at Glastonbury but a morning tweet of "Stoked for Manchester YES!!!!" showed her excitement to be playing here but may have sent some fans hurrying to the wrong venue. She wasn't to be disappointed. Near the end of the set a whispered "This is so cool" to the band showed how much she was loving the experience.

A chance meeting with Jack White had led to his endorsement and now he acts as her mentor. Mattiel's own assessment of her talent can be less than glowing. She has never liked being the centre of attention and on her vocal style "I don't have a traditional singing voice. Someone who is a great singer can be really boring" Take that Jose Carreras, Alexander Armstrong and Nick Knowles. Somewhere in leafy Cheshire Ian Brown's ears were burning 'Hell yeah she's right'

At the end of a top gig, that bouncer who can see over Everest decided he was in a hurry and used Hong Kong police tactics to shoo us out, one of the couple who had been stood next to me said "That was great, thanks for putting up with us. I'm 62 now. What age do you have to stop going to these things?" "Never" She told me that they were from Blackburn and it had a great music scene. I texted a mate who lives there and he simply replied, "You must be joking" Somehow myself, Blackburn and Mattiel hurrying from stage to merch stall managed to avoid being clouted with the crowd control barrier the giant was marching forward with. The Lancastrians stayed in the bar till the last minute then hurried for what must be a great experience the 23.00 to Blackburn.

Two even older lads were at the top bar and completely confusing the trendies by having a great night out, laughing and joking. This isn't cool and neither was that denim jacket.

New barmaid Jenna from Leeds must have been pitched in at the deep end. Completely unaware of Gorilla's protocol. Bar staff should hover near that back door or when in the bar area walk centrally not hearing the squawking on either side, like carrying a bag of chips down Blackpool pier ignoring the seagulls. Jenna was shooting from side to side like a Squash player. No! That is just wrong. It was Jenna's first night, she will learn from experience.

Tonight, Brad Pitt barman had got lucky and was being chatted up by a New Yorker. You could see the exact moment she engaged her prey. Lippy was applied, deep breath and hair tousled. The way American girls talk that was him out of action for the rest of the shift. Jenna toiled on.

Raven haired beauty (her of the crop tops) then made an appearance dressed to kill as she was heading out for the night. Only a cursory inspection to see if maybe there was a model agency talent spotter in or Maxine Peake's new workshop's casting director. Quality gig by Mattiel, she will be back, but did Jenna make her second shift, or had she burned out?

Top Tune: Mattiel "Count your blessings"

Mattiel Brown

Meatballs on the tram

Can't be sure exactly where he emerged from but probably that cave near Trafford Bar station. He introduced himself to the late-night Airport tram by dropping a three quarters full can of Stella on the floor. What a noise it made, caught everyone's attention. He looked not unlike the convict in the original Great Expectations. Audible dismay and fear spread down the tram. A record number of people got off at Firswood. Sat with my back to him could hear the oncoming slobbering and knew my turn was coming. Tactics are all important, take control. He spouted something that would have needed subtitles for a Neanderthal. I said firmly "I've no idea what you're saying mate" He replied even more firmly "F**kin meatball" and walked off. Yep I thought, proud of myself, handled that well. He sat on a recently vacated seat, dropped the can again, grunted something emotional and burst into tears. The anti-social Police nabbed him further down the line. A second wave of inspectors got on later in a Metrolink charm offensive and I told one "That lunatic they threw off called me a meatball, what does that mean?" Chuckling uncontrollably, he shouted to his mate "Oi Tony. What does meatball mean?" 'Faggot' was Tony's cheery reply. They were still laughing when I got off and one of them shouted "Have a good night mate" Felt so small when I got home, I went in through the cat flap.

Tramlines

It looked like 50 years of marriage had taken its toll. Sat almost grudgingly next to each other there wasn't much left to say. Five stops of silence staring straight ahead. Then in between Moor Rd and Wythenshawe Park she spotted that speed boat on the drive "Ooh look must have been a Bullseye contestant" Involuntary twitch from him. No way he was going to giggle.

Sometimes you can get awkward conversations when thrown together on the tram. One Saturday morning saw a woman I hadn't seen for decades taking her elderly dad for breakfast at the Forum. She was far more adept at casual conversation than me and getting off she managed to fit in the weather, family days out and the excitement of a weekend fry up. "Bye see you have a good day at work" I waved but just couldn't think of anything to reply and blurted out "Yep see you. Enjoy that breakfast. Two fried eggs!" Glad them doors close quickly.

It is such a long journey on that tram to town they should spice up the station names with a few local phrases to let you know exactly where you are. A woman got on at Baguley, phone clamped to her ear and her little daughter on reins. As the tram lurched slightly going downhill the poor child fell forward on to hands and knees and burst out crying. Mum only paused her conversation to say "Shaddup you weirdo" 'The next stop will be Moor Road. Shaddup you weirdo'

To let you know you have entered another county, I once heard a couple getting on at St Werburgh's, in the middle of a chasm deep artsy conversation. She had him stumped with a difficult question about the name of a film, and he had to adjust his pretentious cap to play for more time 'The next stop will be Chorlton. Is that Luc Besson's work'

Naked Ambition

There are many schools of thought over what truly signalled the end of civilisation. Another series of Naked Ambition being commissioned is one. Surely Cilla in all them series of Blind Date never had to utter the phrase "Ooh I bet that piercing brought tears to your eyes chuck" Can you imagine David Bowie when he fell to earth and put all them tellys on and this was on every channel? Disturbing. There seems for some reason to be an inordinate number of bus drivers who take part. As yet not many people of the cloth though I believe the Newsnight vicar is being considered for the next series. If not working for Stagecoach most of the other contestants seem to work in retail especially Aldi. So, what does happen after you've made an appearance on the show. Aldi canteen, Monday morning. "Did you do anything over the weekend?" "No, I was too tired" "Nice weather we had a walk in the Peak District" "I was on that Naked Ambition" "I thought that was you. Didn't know you had a tattoo, is it an armadillo?" "No, it's a peacock I had it done 20 years ago"

A close runner up must be the hide behind the couch toe curling Love Island that has only ever been enlivened by the interviewing technique of Caroline Flack "You're an underwear model, you read books, you cook! What can't you do?"

Sofar Sounds is such a brilliant concept. New bands playing cool and unusual venues to hip chicks and dudes (and on this occasion two others) Tonight we are at Thoughtworks, in an office block just off Dantzic St. I've gone with my mate D a resident of Chorlton town. He has usually had a couple of herbal teas (made from leaves smuggled from the slopes of Machu Pichu) before leaving the house. These are unlicensed, bring a bottle or two nights and I've only brought a few which I had sourced from the superb Beermoth on Tib St. Shockingly he turns up sober and we've soon gone through our stash. Frustrating. D then disappeared off and came wandering back with one bottle of lager. One bottle! Never ever do a Brinks-Mat with this man "I've got mine Cheers"

Tonight's bands: James Bradshaw (ex-Michael Buble tribute act on the northern circuit) Chloe Foy (Gloucester songstress, just had a wisdom tooth out) and A. Wesley Chung (Californian in Glasgow)

It later turned out that Mr Chung had left the bottle on the side while he went to the toilet. Apologies Wesley.

At a later Sofar gig at Base Manchester I was one of the last three to arrive as an O2 breakdown had almost paralysed the western world. Was greeted by a lovely lady on the door who ticked me off the list, smiled and said "Welcome, we have biscuits" 'Cheers I love a biscuit' and took three. When I looked back at her that welcoming expression had changed to 'That's one biscuit each dickhead' They were lovely sort of Turkish Delight meets marshmallow.

Favourite Sofar tunes on YouTube Findlay "Waste my time" Andreya Triana "That's alright with me"

Light Bites

The Old Abbey used to be a staging post on the rollicking jaunt from the city centre to Maine Rd on derby day. Today it's slap bang in the middle of the University Science Park. A pretty funky beer garden and an extreme stripped back look inside. The kind of stripping back that a beaver might do. A fantastic pizza review had brought me here and a genuine one from a real person not from one of Gordo's mates.

Somehow the barmaid had teleported here all the way from Colorado. I bet that was a far more interesting story than this afternoon's other 3 customers could tell. Two blokes sat in the corner with a dog on a rope. They were discussing alternative meanings of the afterlife provided by sci fi films. Every now and again the dog would try and join in the conversation. I think he was saying "Please no not this again" Out of the three he looked least like Chewbacca.

I ordered the only non-veggie pizza and Colorado warned it would be a bit of a wait. That was because they had to call the emergency meat eating chef in to handle the chicken.

The eco warriors trundled off to watch some films and were replaced by two friends, a lad and girl. He had purple streaks in his hair and was waiting excitedly for his girlfriend to arrive.

When she did arrive, he greeted her with "Wow. How many thousands of awesome points have you scored today?" If the dog had still been here, he would have said "Yikes" Fairly unique place.

Pizza 5/5 Ale 4/5 Decor 3/5 Dog Conversation 2/5 Chat up line 0/5

Northern Soul Grilled Cheese

Can there be a better Mancunian experience than sitting in the Northern Soul shack on Church St watching the world struggle past in driving rain while you are eating the Tandoori Special 3 cheese toastie? Superbly accompanied by a perfectly vinegared gherkin, red cabbage, dandelion and burdock and Jnr Walker. Perfect. Warning, if you have lived in Manchester all your life and hear of a new place name be very wary. The wild eyed, lights on but nobody home expressions on the buses passing by to Holts Estate. What cruel human experiments are being conducted there? Top Tune: "Mama told me..." The Shirelles

Nilufer Yanya

The perfect sound for a summer's night. Indie with a huge dollop of soul. Who could resist someone with the name Nilufer Yanya? Turkish, Irish and Bajan heritage and from a family of musicians and performers. Her nan is a massive music fan, Irish trad one day and Bob Marley the next. Add in Nilufer's own influences Elliott Smith and Nina Simone and you have a huge mixed palette to work with.

The gig came at a time when the tensions between the two fat boys in the playground Trump and Kim Jong-un had thankfully eased but the #metoo crisis was at its height. On a baking hot evening a stunning Oriental lady was striding down Oxford Rd just near All Saints Park. Sunglasses on top of her head, bright red dress, fantastic walk. What could possibly go wrong? The dress had snagged in her belt at the back. What if English wasn't her first language who dared walk up and point at her derriere? What if there were rad femmes watching from the park? Confusion and hesitancy. What would Donald have done? Luckily at the Pelican Crossing a student girl stepped in, repairs done and by the time they had reached the other side of the road they were best friends. Easy.

Nilufer was without doubt the coolest person in Manchester tonight. Despite admitting she finds it difficult to adjust to playing in front of big crowds, she bounds on stage with glee. For a mere novice she hides her nerves well and seems totally at ease. She came to prominence at open mic nights in London, has featured on that C4 music programme they hide after midnight and was named by 6music as one of the Sounds of 2018. Creative unfussy tunes, almost sparse at times and she definitely has not yet been forced down any musical cul de sac. The beauty is in the simplicity. You wouldn't want an over keen producer to get anywhere near her songs. Add to that a really individual guitar playing style that mesmerises and this is glorious stuff. Great rapport with bandmate Jazzi Bobbi. Unlike Nilufer I'm pretty sure that's not her real name unless she's from an even more musical family.

All too soon, repertoire complete, she is gone. At only 23 there is so much more to come. She will be back many times. Future star. Top Tunes: "Small Crimes"" Heavyweight Champion of the Year""Paradise" and Pixies cover "Hey" Nilufer Yanya

Nine Below Zero, Yo La Tengo

Somewhere in the loft is the bright green vinyl of the classic 1981 Nine Below Zero album 'Don't point your finger'. Dennis Greaves and Mark Feltham have been playing RnB together for nearly 40 years. Tonight, they are rocking the life out of Club Academy, the best Academy by far. Plenty of rock chicks have made the effort and are rocking the leather trousers and high heels look. The band are rocking more of a beer belly and receding hairline look. Thankfully they've recruited support act Charlie Austen to sing backing vocals in a tiny red frock. That deflected most people's attention. That's Charlie Austen of Lux Lisbon and not Charlie Austin the burly bearded Southampton striker. Thank God.

A great night out. The only down point for singer Dennis is the antics of his son who is also a band member. Dennis had shown him round his favourite Manchester haunts in the day prompting his son to say, "You know dad I think I prefer Manchester to London" As Dennis says "That's just not right for a Bermondsey boy"

Top Tunes: "Tore Down" Nine Below Zero "Traces of You" Charlie Austen "Animals" Lux Lisbon

You really need to see a band live to appreciate what they are all about. Yo La Tengo have stayed around longer than Cliff at a royal garden party. Their first album was released in 1986 and they have been a big part of many people's lives since then. If you look at comments on YouTube it is full of "Thanks YLT you have helped me through so much of my adult life"

The pride on the faces of the crowd as their heroes took to the stage, some almost tearful. The band are definitely not everyone's cup of tea but are considered musician's musicians. As a TV presenter they would be a Philip Schofield/Richard Madeley mash up.

The first half was so shoe gaze I got tired of looking at mine and started looking at everyone else's. I wasn't quite feeling it unlike the schmoozing young couple in front who were exchanging more than compliments. I edged cringingly away from the lovebirds towards the fire exit manoeuvring my coat on the floor with my left foot, like Maradona with a brandy in his hand. The security woman on the door didn't look impressed by the skill. After only a few songs, our vigilant security leader quietly eased back on the door, arms outstretched. I thought wow, that's an extravagant rest. This shoe gaze is some relaxant. Luckily the fire door had those sorts of pedals for handles and not the steel bar. The pedals lodged in her yellow jacket and held her up. I was none the wiser, the lovers were oblivious. Thankfully one young lad passing by was more observant and eased her off the pedals towards the floor. I managed to left foot my Berghaus right under her head as they laid her down. What a great job the young lad did and within seconds another kind heart was there with a soothing cold cloth and glass of water. With help from bar staff they soon had her sitting. All superstars apart from that one loudmouth bellowing "Get her in the recovery" Does he attend all incidents?

It was just a dizzy spell and the young heroes returned to work or watching music as more security staff arrived to look after her. When the St John's Ambulance arrived, he tapped me on the shoulder and said "Cheers. Well done mate. Thanks so much" He must have seen that left footed artistry. Unwarranted plaudits. Surely, he could have got his hand in his pocket for another Cognac. Sadly, for the security lady it was only after she'd been subbed that the gig improved hugely.

At five past ten they played "Nothing to hide" and from then on, the place was rocking. One of those gigs that suddenly burst into life and you never know when it will end. This caught out the bloke in the brown leather jacket with the combover. He was just turning from the bar with 3 pints in his hands when it was suddenly all over. He had no means of clapping or wiping away a tear. Emotional.

Top Tune: "For you too" Yo La Tengo

NBZ & Charlie

No Record Player

"Music can transport you. Like a fly accidentally getting stuck in the tour bus and ending up 200 miles from home" Cate le Bon 6Music interview September 2019, probably nailing the rock lunatic of the year title. Have always had a soft spot for mad women in music since seeing Lene Lovich wearing her gran's curtains on Top of the Pops. Back in 2016 had seen Julia Holter play Manchester Cathedral and thought her impressively bonkers. That is until she showed up in Stevenson Square this year with her boyfriend Tashi Wada and his merry band. Any gig that promises bagpipe solos sounds special to me. The Tashi Wada Group featuring Julia Holter and Corey Fogel. Try fitting that on a traditional drum kit.

Support artist Kepla certainly fitted the unconventional vibe. He stayed crouched over his work desk with the intensity of a NASA scientist analysing data from another Galaxy. I had been joined on the school benches at the side of Soup Kitchen's basement by a Wirral schoolteacher and her husband. They were committed Mancophiles apparently and always making the journey east for gigs. We agreed this electronic symphony was fascinating but would never make it on to Now That's What I Call Music 110. I asked the husband "How do you go about memorising something like that?" 'Make it up as you go along'

She was definitely the cougar and he the toy boy. The first sign of M62 tension came when she declared that she had loved The Hacienda. I said "No, you could never cop off, everyone was way too..." 'No, they weren't, yes you could' We found common ground on all being fans of The Fall. I asked if they knew a brawl had broken out at Mark's funeral and maybe that would have made him laugh. She was outraged and waded in with "Mancs are such dickheads. My friend lives here and loves it but hates the Mancs" I nearly dropped my JD. Then she tried some diplomacy. "Scousers are dickheads as well" Who knew schoolteachers were this controversial? Yoshi and Julia were just making their way on stage. "Are we standing up? I know I am" and off she went with toy boy in tow.

A Sunday night gig with no work in the morning is a thing of beauty. Everyone else was having a quiet one, where I could radically overindulge and basically baste myself in Jack Daniels. This made a moment before the music started even more enjoyable. Master percussionist Corey had been rummaging through his bag on the side of the stage. As he looked up, he banged his head on the huge gong at the side of the drumkit. You rang. Thankfully Toshi had kept the bagpipe track in the set. As a creative couple how had he broached this to Julia? "I've got this idea for a song" (15 second blast on one bagpipe note) Julia "Work in progress?" T "Yep, work in progress" Julia "Don't give up the day job" "Pardon" "Nothing" On Julia's last album the most accessible track "Turn the Light on" was described by Rolling Stone magazine as "a good kind of apocalypse" The Observer described the whole album Aviary as an 'ordeal' Rapturous ovation from the forty plus 40+ crowd. Julia was greeted at the merch stall by an adoring fan all the way from Mexico. They chatted joyously about a gig at an old church in Mexico City. Some real devotees here. Two clean cut probably teetotal American lads asked me if I was in the merch queue "No just drinking" They watched me finish off the JD with the look of someone watching a horse drinking out of a bucket of water for the first time. The frat pack had a quick word then suddenly I was left with just Julia and Toshi. Not wanting to seem like a cheapskate I said to Julia "Err Can I have an album? I've got nothing to play it on though" J looking at T "Wow people in Manchester are so wow. Hey, buy something to play it on" Toshi began "You know you can download the app off..." then gave up realising it was a lost cause "What's that mate?" With her reputation I was expecting Julia to be a raving lunatic, but she was delightful and really shy.

Julia "We go to Exeter tomorrow. Do you know it?" "Yeah, it's full of bumpkins" "Bun kins?" Tashi asked if they should all sign the album, but I feared the worst when he said, "I will just go get a Sharpie" After they had autographed my £20 album I said "Wow thank you. This will be worth a fortune in the future" Julia who says she suffers from severe impostor syndrome 'I'm so embarrassed asking other musicians to play my songs' furrowed her brow unconvinced.

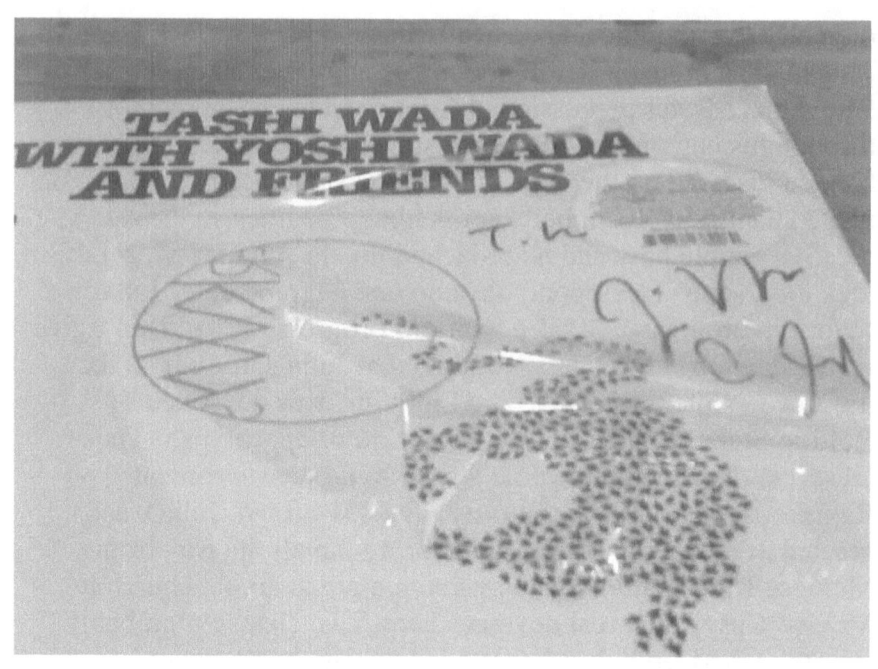

Northern Tennis Club

Watching top class tennis on a summer's day with a pint of
Shipyard. What could possibly go wrong? Apart from Storm
Hector visiting Manchester on a flying visit. American player
Claire Liu clad in designer thermals was officially the coldest
person on the planet. It doesn't help your state of mind when the
service ball toss is nearly blown over the fence onto Palatine Rd.
Brief periods of piercing sunshine in amongst the hurricane winds
and black clouds, wasn't enough to improve the all-round
withered looks and frayed nerves. Claire was playing an at first
smiley Evgeniya Rodina who was far more accustomed to the
Siberian conditions. One comment though from her bearded
hoodie wearing coach changed her mood completely and the ball
boy took a full blast in Russian. His dad was just the other side of
the perimeter fence "Don't listen to her son" A Russian speaking
12-year-old? That's Didsbury educators at their best.
In true British tradition, local favourite and Number 1 seed
Naomi Broady had already gone out. As had the suspiciously

named Luksika Kumkhum who I'm sure was a character in The 40-Year-Old Virgin.

After Rodina's win I was fortunately blown back into the hospitality tent by the gales for more Shipyard and a Northern Soul Panini (Black pudding, tomato, mozzarella and rocket) The ladies next to me were Chicken Caesar Salad Box and Prosecco (from the wonderful Thyme outside caterers). They had just booked a villa on Santorini that slept 16. Fourteen friends! that's just showing off. Santorini doesn't even hold sixteen people.

Top Tune: "Always coming back to you" Hooton Tennis Club
After a few more sets was feeling hungry again. Where to eat on Burton Rd? Like a kid in a sweet shop so much choice. Settled for a window seat at Volta. Whoever did the Feng- shuing at this place got it spot on. A happy vibrant place with genuinely friendly staff. I ordered the 3 small plates for £7.50 and couldn't recognise much on the plates apart from pomegranate. Great food and the barman helpfully informed me that one of the mystery dishes was called Baba Ganoush, the defeated number 13 seed at Northern. There was a Thursday afternoon understated hen party in. One delightful hen in tiara with two friends. A far more acceptable number of buddies. Maybe too many Shipyards but I was just about to leave when the chicken skewers arrived. Surely, I can count to 3 or 40. Advantage me.

Definitely would never make it as an umpire.

Another favourite V you can't go wrong with is Vapiano, in the foodie mecca of the Corn Exchange. This is the place where you get a little clocking in card and then use it to tot up your bill. You swipe at the counter as the chef prepares your meal in front of you. True fast food of great quality. The concept was obviously devised by a cunning Italian chef so he could chat up the ladies. My conversation with a bearded Neapolitan chef was therefore brief "Which pasta?" "Penne" "Extra chillies. Extra cheese. More garlic?" "Oh yes" Gamberetti y spinaci with extra everything, and it was superb. Top food and an army of attentive staff. Highly recommended.

Oh Hellos

The barman looked so proud after managing to serve a large group of potentially problematic Americans. Fussing about looking at every bar pump they all eventually settled on a Brooklyn. Phew. Relieved he turned to the next customer, a young local girl and she asked for a Gin Sprite. Everybody 'A what?' The staff in BOTW are here for the music not an audition in Cocktail II.

Tonight, brother and sister Taylor and Maggie Heath have brought along seven bandmates all the way from San Marcos, Texas. Collectively they are known as The Oh Hellos and truly you will never meet a happier band. The Oh Hellos have no connection with English cad Leslie Phillips and are definitely no relation to Marc Riley's favourite band Thee Oh Sees

Whoever said you can always trust a large band because they are in it for love not money was right. Strangely, though Tyler keeps talking about the nine of them, I can still only spot eight, no matter how few Warsteiner I'd had. Surely, they hadn't left one in the extra-large tour van. Special mention to the guitarist in the baseball cap who genuinely seemed to be having the night of his life.

A really infectious laid-back sound with effortless harmonies. Like a Texan porch on a Sunday night. The enthusiasm of one mass singalong to 'Exeunt' stopped the band in its tracks. Then the percussionist slowly eased himself into the crowd rather than surfed onto it. After some jigging about he clambered back on stage with a grin. He revealed he had asked two lads "Can you pick me up now?" and one of them replied "Why?"

Unable to contain a huge smile, Tyler took a time out and said to the band just loud enough for all of us to hear "Nearly half way there now, we can do this" Then turning back to the crowd "We can all do this" Later minus the rest of the band he and Megan did the encore alone and admitted "This is terrifying"

On a Tuesday night in a barren January, this was an absolute gem. If you couldn't enjoy this, you need to reboot your soul. As we were leaving there was a sea of beaming faces in the bar waiting to greet their eight or nine heroes. Priceless.

Top Tune; "Hello my old heart" The Oh Hellos

Old Fashioned Curry

Had to pay a visit to St Peter's Square to see Hazel Reeves's brilliant Mrs Pankhurst statue. When I made the pilgrimage there was an elderly couple gazing at her just totally besotted. Proud smiling faces as they snapped away taking an album full of photos. Couldn't resist a "Is it Mrs May?" He was the much smaller of the two and grinned but with the rider of "Oh no what have you said?" She had the look of Tyson Fury climbing off the canvass in the 12th round. Suddenly Anthology. looked hugely appealing and I escaped in there before taking a left hook from a 75-year-old.

What a great view this bar has. The bustle of people and trams flowing in and out of the square with the back view of Central Library and The Midland. This really should be the official centre of the city.

Outstanding people watching spot, the Martin Mere of humans. Was sure I'd heard Anthology mentioned as one of the top purveyors of an Old Fashioned in Manchester. Looking at the cocktail menu was relieved it was made with Bulleit Bourbon and not the much-favoured Woodford Reserve. I asked the barman how to pronounce it and he said, 'as from a gun' Sounded much more sinister in his Bulgarian accent. The only bullet holes in here would come from the firing of Prosecco corks at the weekend hen dos. Angostura bitters, orange peel and brown sugar, hugely enjoyable. Helpfully if you have one too many, the bar has left little clusters of vintage books on each table to remind you of where you are drinking. This works well in here but wouldn't be the same in the two pubs local to me. In the Red Beret, you wouldn't want to find a load of old scarlet felt hats on the table and even less so in the Cornishman.

Another listed Old Fashioned comes from the Bollibar at Asha's glitzy restaurant on Peter Street. High class venue and varied menu but after a heavy on wallet and waistline Christmas settled for the basic 3 course meal deal which had half a pint of bitter thrown in. Really loved the seafood kebab and jalfrezi. Outstanding. These posh Indian restaurants should be careful about leaving nonedible stuff on the table when a hungry Philistine walks in. That might just have been a house plant I mistook for a side dish. Apologies. Top quality food and enough to feed a small horse. Saw one amazing review on Trip Advisor later that said, "Portion sizes very small" Could only have been Tyson Fury again.

Some heresy here. Asha's take on the Old Fashioned is the New Fashioned and features rum and not whiskey or bourbon. Mixed with orange, muscovado sugar and all spice, really wanted to hate it but it was brilliant.

Top waitress Millie was not from a distant Punjab village but from the much closer Poznan. I said, "Ah Lech Poznan" and she said, "How would you even know that?" She was not to be intimidated by the Brexit stormtroopers. Determined this was her new home and new life. Wonderful, I will drink to that.

A more recent addition to the Manc curry scene is the long anticipated Dishoom in the palatial surroundings of the 1920's masonic hall on Bridge Street. Amazing surroundings .Both staff and customers just seem excited to be here. Timing affects everything. Thanks to TfGM (bus stuck on tram tracks at Baguley) had arrived 5 minutes too late for the Bombay Breakfast (bacon on naan bread). Not knowing I'd arrived directly between sittings I asked the woman on the fancy reception "Do you have a table for one?" "Oh, go on then, only because it's you" The place was briefly totally empty, but this meant I got the full attention of the lovely waitress from way darn south. She had moved north with Hawksmoor but had either been head hunted or free transferred to Dishoom. She patiently explained the full menu to me with recommendations as the place filled up with an expectant lunchtime throng. Loved her choices and was much taken by the décor and especially them ceiling fans. Special mention to the luscious black daal, perfect roti and a healthy portion of Gulab Jamun.

She even threw in a free cardamom tea. This stuff has a cure all reputation and certainly has a calming influence. Brilliant food. I told the waitress I would study Indian street food and come back a bit wiser. She said "Come back and try everything"

Less conviviality on the way out. I held the door for two warpainted, Primark bagged, Salford lovelies as they dithered over whether to go in or not. They must have thought they were Leadsom and McVey. After I'd stood for a couple of seconds one of them said "You can go now!" Only the cardamom stopped the clever pithy reply I'd thought of. Did they think I was the punka waller? Me too!

After that bout of speed dating needed another Old Fashioned. Headed down the little alley by Neighbourhood and over to The Alchemist. Great instant service. The barman said "Have you been in Alchemist before? Maybe you'd like to try our Smokey Old Fashioned?" " Yeah go right ahead" He mixed it in a chemistry class beaker and then got a flame thrower out and set it on fire "Err that's fantastic" Doing that double clicking sound you encourage horses with and firing an imaginary James Bond handgun he said "Hey if you like it, the name's Matt" and off he went. Overwhelmingly determined to dislike it this time. I couldn't it tasted superb. Like getting drunk at a bonfire. Wouldn't recommend setting fire to someone's drink in The Old Monkey though.

Ole's Finest Hour (PSG 1v3 Man Utd)

Trying to convince friends that Belleville was now the place to stay in Paris. Quoting from a guidebook, I told them it was once known as a gritty insular suburb, not tolerant of outsiders, long associated with rebellion and uprisings. The locals even had their own baffling form of Parisian slang. Not phased at all by that. Reading on "These days it attracts a much younger student crowd and there is a recently formed alliance of over 250 local artists" Looks of dismay "I'm not staying there" "Why not?" "Not if it's full of artists"

Finally, only me and young O made it to the Airbnb on Rue de Belleville. Had some lovely messages from owner Ann who explained the family would be away on holiday that week, but her teenage daughter Moira would stay behind to hand over the keys. When we got there Moira had her two friends with her, all leather trousers and pouts, specifically to see what Manchester football fans looked like. After a liquid journey via Euston and then Eurostar would like to think we didn't disappoint. They were not impressed. Vive la difference.

Before Moira left to join the family in Normandy, she showed us around and introduced us to our two hairy house mates, Storm and Charlie, mother and son, Ann's cats. "Will you be able to look after them?" Stock answer. "Yes, of course" Everything went well until Storm went out for the night and didn't return home for 36 hours.

Charlie didn't seem that concerned but while she was out, we were panicking. Sat in a bar in Pigalle we even considered the Meet the Fockers option. Buy a new one. The pub manager had lived in Australia for a while and so far, had paid scant attention to our conversation and used her English sparingly. Now with eyes narrowed you could easily mistake me and O for relatives, and her eyes had definitely narrowed! After earwigging the conversation, she exploded with full Gallic indignation "What? You would go home and tell the wife. I've lost the son but bought another one to replace him"

What a moment when Storm ambled back in. Charlie just gave a shrug. Without a hint of confidence or hindsight I sold my ticket to another mate for a cut price 50 Euros and watched the game on a pub telly. Rashford slammed in a last-minute penalty. Glorious mayhem.

I thanked the owners for our stay on the Airbnb website and they replied, "Long live Manchester" and Storm.

Tune: The Go Betweens "Finding You"

Charlie with his paws up

Ordsall Hall

There can barely be a more surprising site when out on a Sunday constitutional than Ordsall Hall coming into view sat proudly in its own grounds between gritty housing estate and scenic warehouse park. There has been some form of dwelling here since 1170 when Ordeshala was noted to be paying a feudal tax. A house has definitely been on this site from 1250 when an early employee of Reeds Rains described the view from a riverside window "The house is sheltered in a sweeping bend of the clear waters of the Irwell, where leaping salmon and trout can be seen. All around we are surrounded by vast areas of arable land and meadow. The house has its own stables, granary, dovecote, orchard and windmill" Rural bliss in Salford.

Over the years it has had a fantastic wide range of uses and residents. The noble Radclyffe family called it home for over 300 years. The original Sir John was a war hero who had fought bravely in France at the battle of Crecy (1346). In recognition of service to his country he was allowed to bring back some highly skilled Flemish Weavers (what a pub that was!) to Salford. Their aim was to set up shop here and train the locals. Sir John can rightly be regarded as the founder of the textile industry in Lancashire. By the time the Industrial Revolution exploded into life, Salford had a few generations of skilled workers.

Margaret Radclyffe (1573-99) moved in the upper echelons of society and became the favourite maid of honour to Queen Elizabeth. Renowned for her stunning looks she was known to swan around in £180 frocks. She died of a broken heart, unable to cope with the loss of her twin brother in battle. Playwright and poet Ben Jonson wrote an epigram to her virtue and beauty and Margaret was buried in St Margaret's church in Westminster.

The Radcliffe's association with the house only ended in 1602 and it passed through many other Lancashire land owning families including the Oldfields, the Hattons and the Egertons. An incestuous bunch these property magnates so it can also be linked through marriage with the Booths, Leghs and de Traffords. Some fine names there for local roads, pubs, districts and supermarkets.

Pre-Raphaelite artist, Frederick Shields (1833-1911), was a one-time tenant of the Hall and he described it in a letter to his friend John Ruskin as "the cosiest place I have ever nested" Famous Yorkshire skin and hide merchants, the Markendales made Ordsall Hall their home for much of the 19C. They brought with them from Skipton their own butchers establishing a tradition of skilled local meat cleaver swingers.

This imposing place has had a myriad of uses, seminary, working men's club, air raid warning centre, antique shop and radio station. At one time it even housed Ordsall Job Centre and the clients formed their own football team. That was one side you didn't want to draw in the Salford Sunday Cup. Today it is a hugely popular place for visitors though over the years there have been less complimentary reviews than those of Fred Shields and Reeds Rains.

Dutch thinker Erasmus stayed here in 1499 and described the unique flooring as "made of clay, covered with constantly replenished layers of rushes, spittle, vomit, the urine of dogs and men, the dregs of beer and the remains of fish" He had a think about it and didn't come back. That Trip Advisor review would today bring an instant retort from the Hall's management. In 1895 the Salford Weekly described the house's prevailing odours as being of "fried fish, engine oil and gin" A tradition that was still being carried on nearly a century later just down the road at Liners (Dockers Bar) What a pub that was!

After all this time and so many comings and goings it would be disappointing if the Hall hadn't retained the odd spirit. This being Salford it has at least three. There is cheery child ghost Cecily who comes out to play when she hears a party of school children arrive. Courtier Margaret "The White Lady" still roams the buildings and grounds. Her white gown and floating candle are often seen as she waits anxiously for her brother's return. In the Star Chamber bedroom, cold spots betray the breath of raunchy old goat Sir John. Unwelcome male visitors often feel they are being pushed out whilst female guests have reported a cheeky pinch or squeeze. Historically it can be a dangerous thing to pinch an Ordsall woman.

Tour guides don't tend to last long. It would pay to have eyes in the back of your head. One new employee found the word 'Beware' scrawled in ghostly hand in her new notepad when she turned her back.

All in all, a great place to visit. The staff are lovely, and you can watch fascinating informative historical videos. The building itself still retains the hallmarks of many architectural styles with its Tudor beams, stained glass windows and IKEA gas fires. Wherever I went in the building I kept bumping into the same two ladies. Pretty sure they weren't anything spectral as they said they were from Walkden and Bolton. Walkden thought the 'sympathetic refurb' was maybe a bit too modern and recommended a visit to Smithills, Bolton. Maybe she would have preferred it when Erasmus visited.

I literally bumped into them on the staircase down from the attic, apologised and said I had a damaged Achilles tendon and couldn't balance. Mysteriously they appeared at least twice more emerging from hidden entrances or alcoves as I did the tour of the house. I lost them for a bit but then as I was leaving heard a shout from the coffee shop "Bye, nice to meet you, look after that Hercules tendon"

Osaka Ramones

On this evidence it's healthier being in a punk band than being a punk. Hard gigging, globetrotting Shonan Knife look fantastic belying all the years on the road which can't be said of the crowd. There were more walking sticks than your local A&E. The nackered one next to me was wheezing and hobbling about. A woman who knew him came over and he asked her "Have you ever had sciatica? I'm in agony" Let's rock. Pogo no go zone. He whinged all the way through the support band, Proto Idiot. Naoko Yamano set up Shonan Knife in 1981 with her sister after becoming bored with her humdrum life in Osaka. Her two inspirations were The Ramones and The Buzzcocks. They have been going so long that a one-time childhood groupie Risa Kawano is now the bands drummer.

Risa's English is good and acknowledging the debt to Pete Shelley's boys she said "We are so happy to be here in rock city. Manchester" That devil's horn rock gesture had never looked so joyful or so charming. "We had noodles for lunch, they are so good in Manchester. Not so good in Japan" They then launched into old fave "All you can eat"

Over the years they have had many high-profile admirers. They once supported Sonic Youth on tour. Another fan Kurt Cobain proclaimed them the coolest band on the planet. The Nirvana legend said "Shonan Knife make you happy. I turned into a 9-year-old girl at a Beatles concert. Amazing. I've never been so thrilled in my whole life"

Many people from this era remember XTC's "Making plans for Nigel" but how many can recall "Making plans for bison" the Shonan's unofficial save the wildlife anthem 'Bear up bison,

146

never say die' They finished with a tune from one of their heroes, Nick Lowe. "Cruel to be kind" Great ovation and as a delighted crowd limped away someone said "What just happened there, that was brilliant"

Top Tune: "Tomato Head" Shonan Knife

Manc Albums (d)

(16) Comedian's brother "Turtle Soup" 1990
(17) Oldham dance/punk "X marks destination" 2008
(18) Macclesfield alt-pop debut "This word and body" 1996
(19) Harrogate via Manchester "Wah wah" 1994
(20) 3-piece rock legends "Gods and monsters" 2005

Oshun

You can't beat a random gig booked at the last moment. Someone you have absolutely no knowledge or preconceptions of. Had seen the name Oshun on two lists of gigs not to miss in May 2018. Had never heard of them and thought they could be an indie band from Craggy Island. Wrong by the width of an ocean, they are in fact a hip-hop duo from New York via Washington. My knowledge of hip hop is up there with my knowledge of quantum physics, so had no idea what to expect.

Some strange glances in the Soup Kitchen queue. The three girls in front dressed in variations of those high waisted candy-striped trousers with even higher hair seemed to be debating whether to tell me this wasn't the Post Office queue. The couple in front of them could have been in Deee Lite and looked like they'd recognised their old Physics teacher.

I slunk in and estimated I was the oldest there by about 30 years. Not even a grizzled old bouncer to save the day. Somehow it worked to my advantage and it was easy to get my Mackeson at the bar as everyone was in such good humour and very polite to their elders. Was still expecting a gentle tap on the shoulder and a friendly "Did you get a little lost?"

Oshun are named after a West African goddess and are in fact a Nubian neo soul hip hop collaborative or so at least the music papers say. I settled in the very dark corner at the back like the ghost of Joe Loss.

The sheer energy of Thandi and Niambi was mesmerising and simply blew you away. Their movement, interaction and vocal skills were brilliant. The adoration of the all dancing crowd (all but one) was incredible. What a joyful experience. If any indie band got this kind of reception their heads would never deflate. When Thandi said "There is an awful lot of love in the house tonight" she was seriously understating it. This had real soul, an awesome performance.

Top Tune: "My World" Oshun (with or without Jorja Smith)

A mother's love

We all do our best to ignore the march of time, even when it's marched all over you. Visiting my mother after having a haircut I was bemoaning the amount of grey hair I'd left on the barber's shop floor. She said, "Oh I don't know I think men with grey hair can look quite extinguished" Correct.

Over Expectations

The prolific and brilliant singer songwriter Laura Marling had teamed up with Mike Lindsay of Tunng to form Lump. The result was described as avant-garde folk. One of those three letter expressions that strikes terror into your heart like Eccles Beer Festival or Jacob Rees-Mogg.

Full marks to the pair of them for the experimentation but this has the trajectory of a Chris Waddle penalty. 'Late to the Flight' details a man's premonition of his imminent death "So don't wear your smiley face t-shirt tonight"

The band do make some original industrial type buzzing sounds with Laura's beautiful voice floating over the top of them. It's a bit like champagne with a vindaloo. One newspaper didn't curry favour in its sparse review. Two of the kinder words were 'pretentious' and 'claptrap'. The Band on the Wall's marketing team tried its best and were keen to point out that Lump was an actual being, a yeti like creature that had passed through both Laura and Mike. Another Warsteiner please.

For anybody in Manchester who has ever been tempted to drunkenly don a Guinness hat on St Patrick's day, Toss the Feathers will always hold a place in your heart. Blasting out their raucous brand of folk rock in Levenshulme pubs, The International, St Kentigerns, or Paddy Crerand's 'Park'. An absolute joy.

For a night celebrating 150 years of the TUC, Desi and Mike are back together for a one-off gig at The Mechanic's Institute on Princess St. The very best Irish fiddle and flute players you will ever find. Fittingly the Mechanics has a staircase very similar to Croagh Patrick so most of the crowd opt for the lift. Fantastic musicianship and an in-depth introduction to each set of tunes. Irish music in a serious almost classical form. No di diddly eye di. Before long you were crying out for a melodeon, bodhrán or someone crashing out of a drunken Siege of Ennis.

After a sedate first half punctuated by a smattering of polite applause Desi sensed the mood "After the interval we are going to play some more popular stuff" A female voice shouted back "Hope so" They didn't. In the old days band and crowd would all have decamped to O'Sheas afterwards for a few nightcaps. Only four of us made the short trip. Time moves on.

Top Tune "Nostalgia" The Chameleons

Sometimes no expectations at all are best. Once I met a wonderful young Hannover couple who were delighted to have flown over for ten euros each. They definitely were sharing some secret. Really hope they had eloped, nobody should look that happy at Cornbrook station. Thinking they would have splashed out on expensive accommodation I asked where they were staying. Getting his phone out he was struggling to remember "Err it is Shudhill? Lower Turk's Head. Is it good?" Now it was my turn to be delighted. She looked happy and puzzled "Can you recommend anywhere?" "Just stay in there or go next door to the Hare and Hounds, you will see all life" They went on their merry way. Fantastic

In its opening week had a tremendous meal at one of them new designer kebab restaurants that had left me salivating every time I walked by since. Couldn't resist going back in early one Tuesday afternoon as apparently I had missed a trick. The flatbreads here were the greatest on earth (Trip Advisor) Very few in but a manager grinning inanely at his laptop, probably writing reviews. Eagerly ordered some hummus with a flat bread for a starter and it tasted like Apollo 13's heatshield. Maybe just bad timing.

Peveril Pub Quiz

After arriving late, I signed up with Liam who suspiciously also didn't have a team. Quizmaster Matt assured me this was a good idea as Liam was a Japanese speaking, Chemical Engineering student and all-round boffin. Added to my moderate knowledge of obscure sporting achievements we could be an outside bet for the title.

Early doors things looked promising as we dredged up the names of obscure Irish rivers, Grand National winners and the dark corners of the Periodic Table. Without warning all four wheels came spinning off. Up to now I had deferred to his impressive educational qualifications. Then came the question "What do the letters AONB stand for?" Without hesitation, Liam 'Atlantic

Ordnance Nuclear Bunker' 'Is that the right answer?' 'I don't know but it's 4 words that begin with them letters' This was getting difficult, what was he drinking, Stella and Sake chasers? "Which country has 4 different vowels in it?" L perplexed head in hands 'What's up?' 'I'm trying to get Azerbaijan' 'It's only got 3' 'I know but I think it's spelt different over there" What was he smoking? "What was the most common female Christian name in Victorian times?" "Mary" "How do you know that?' 'It's my mother's name" "What? How old is your mam" 'She's very old' It was right!

We were languishing in bottom place and crying out for help when the picture round began. Women are brilliant at spotting likenesses, so we stopped an innocent non team member on her way to the toilet. She said, "Definitely number 13 is Mo Farah" Liam "I disagree I was going to say Chris Rock" The only other one our team was agreed on, the heavily bearded man at number 3 was John Lennon. It turned out to be Gerry Adams.

We didn't win any trophies. Liam is a great guy and once pulled me from under a bus on Chepstow St, poured me into a taxi and pointed towards Wythenshawe. Lifesaver and he did get that engineering degree. Just don't ask him what them letters after his name stand for.

Just two weeks later was with my mate B on a quiet pre match drinking afternoon in Mulligans. In true Mulligans style a lad fell spectacularly off the back of his stool, dusted himself off, sat back down and carried on drinking. Not a soul batted an eyelid. Just to his left were a bunch of suits, one of whom looked hugely familiar. Due to the proximity of San Carlo we decided it was a celebrity chef. Months later I saw him on Question Time, it was Paul Mason, former C4 news editor. If we'd had a woman there, she would have got him straight away.

Ten minutes before kick-off we decided to get a taxi to the ground still trying to remember who the celeb was. The taxi driver said "You seem like good guys. Where are you from" "Wythenshawe. You seem like a good guy. Where are you from?" "Pakistan. I have to work all hours of the day to put my son through Uni. He's doing a Chemical Engineering course" That quiz team is beginning to take shape.

Phoebe Bridgers

One of 2017s best albums was Stranger in the Alps by Phoebe Bridgers "I don't think I'll be embarrassed about it in two years' time" No worries there, it's a melancholy masterpiece. She even turns all the studio lights out when recording her vocals to give them that special intimacy. Was first drawn to her after hearing the lines we all could have written "I want to live at the Holiday Inn, where somebody else makes the bed"

The delight on Phoebe's face at the warmth of the Gorilla reception is heart-warming. This is the city that Morrissey's lyrics had taught her so much about. She is amazed by her fans support and really does appreciate them. "Even if you are not in the best of moods, you owe it to the fans to give them the best show you can" After time scrabbling around LA open mic nights and playing to bartenders and empty bar stools, she now sells out all venues. Truly living her dream, she has since recorded with childhood hero Conor Oberst, toured with the wistful Julien Baker and had a liaison with Ryan Adams. The less said about that the better. Maybe just drop a few hints in a song.

Her protective mom is her biggest fan and will happily argue on social media with anyone who dares criticise Phoebe. It was a good job she wasn't here tonight. After three songs, a voice near the front shouted, "The sound is f**kin s***" Total shock from all around. Was this a stunt? A voice from the back replied indignantly but not really helpfully "The sound is f**kin awesome"

Bassist Anna Butters turned open mouthed toward Phoebe. What had they stumbled into here? Who was the lunatic critic and adversary? Had a drunken Ryan Adams stumbled in? He was soon extracted from the crowd and propped up against the small bar behind the stage as they tried to pour iced water into him. Was it just a Tourette's moment? No. He kept on "So I'm not entitled to an opinion then?" Absolutely crackers. Sadly for him he had the stature and look of Bill Oddie and the bouncer on duty was that one who is the size of a Transformer. He did his best to appease the angry ant but then to the amazement of onlookers, Bill lashed out at him. Our favourite Transformer simply caught the tiny fist and frog marched him out the fire door.

He missed a great gig, but nobody missed him. The crowd and band bonded together after that. The incident so bizarre it only left comical memories. Could only be put down to a full moon and hopefully didn't harm Phoebe's view of Manchester. We need her to keep coming back. If she goes back to them Morrissey lyrics, he did kind of warn her that it was a place full of lunatics. Lovely mellow sounds. That emotional but crystal-clear voice over the sparkling guitar and those romantic lyrics that live long in the memory "When a machine keeps me alive and I'm losing all my hair. I hope you kiss my rotten head and pull the plug" Wow. Eat your heart out Ed Sheeran. That is true melancholy for you. Phoebe is only 24. Gig of the year.

Top Tunes: "Killer" "Funeral" "Motion sickness" "Would you rather?" Phoebe Bridgers

and a YouTube gem. Phoebe Bridgers and Noah and Abby Gundersen "Killer and The Sound"

LA Witch are another band who have always bigged up Manchester's music scene. Bassist Irita Pai is another huge fan of Brexit secretary Morrissey. Before their gig at Soup Kitchen she had said "Hearing him sing really conjured up strong images of life in northern England. As a kid growing up in California, it sounded romantic" Morrissey's tentacles stretch very far.

Pip and Vera

One of the sincerest thank yous to a crowd I've ever heard came from Dutch singer Pip Blom. Pip is the daughter of Erwin Blom whose own band Eton Crop were a favourite of John Peel and in the 1980's recorded five Live sessions for him. Her own band are masters of the energetic 3-minute pop barnstormer. They have an infectious love of playing live and could easily conquer the world in 2020. Ace drummer. The last time they played in Manchester at Band on the Wall, Pip said, "Hey thank you all for coming tonight, I know it's the Champions League final" It was Liverpool in the final! And the guitarist added "and the Spice Girls are playing just down the road" It really wasn't a problem for anyone. The morning after Liverpool's 3-0 semi-final first leg defeat to Barcelona, I had gone for a premature celebratory Catalan Migas

in the wonderful Lunya on Deansgate. Only noticed on leaving that the smug texting of friends "In Lunya having breakfast" had auto corrected to "In Libya having breakfast" This would have made far more sense the morning after Pip Blom because Liverpool not only defeated Barcelona on aggregate in the semi they then went on to win the bloody thing. We are not bitter.
The curious case of artist disappointed in crowd. Goth-Country goddess Vera Sola feigned slight dismay as she looked out at the quiet hugely respectful crowd at The Castle. "The last time I played on this street was across the way at Gulliver's as part of the Elvis Perkins band. I've toured all over the world and that was without doubt the rowdiest most drunken crowd I've ever played to" Twice Elvis had asked for requests and both times someone shouted out the title of the song they had just played. Confusing but mild for Gulliver's.
Top Tunes: Pip Blom "I think I'm in Love "Vera Sola "The Colony"

Selfie nation. Pip & friends.

Rapture in Tameside

As far as I can see there have only ever been 2 famous people who were born in or resided in Ashton-under-Lyne. One scored a controversial hat trick in the 1966 World Cup final and the other was the even more controversial prophet, John Wroe.

Ashton had long been known as a hotbed of non-conformity and a religious melting pot. A perfect place for John to settle when he moved over from Yorkshire. He was born in 1782 but he inspired a certain look and mentality still prevalent in Ashton "A man of peculiar appearance who inspired uneducated and wonder loving people with a strange fascination" Faragism.

John set up his church of Christian Israelites and announced that Ashton was a holy city, the new Jerusalem. A citadel in the town centre would be enclosed by four gates, through which the chosen ones would flow. The citadel was a sanctuary where the godly would survive the Apocalypse. One of the gates was the Odd Whim public house. John believed that 10 of the 12 lost tribes of Israel were knocking about somewhere in the North West, probably on Northern Rail.

Always the showman whilst being baptised in the River Aire, near Bradford, he announced like Moses he was about to part the waters. Sadly they refused to budge. John then went way too far by being publicly circumcised at the age of 42. Even Channel 5 turned down the television rights.

In 1830 John claimed that God had messaged him and commanded "Take seven virgins (some accounts say nine. John said the more the merrier) to cherish and comfort you" Local dignitaries seeking publicity scrambled to provide their daughters for a religious tour. When one of them fell pregnant John defended himself by saying "Rejoice for she is in child with my son, the shiloh or messiah" It turned out she had a daughter and the old charlatan was chased out of town.

He resurfaced in Australia (like an early Rod Stewart tour) still surrounded by his long-haired unshaven followers who were known as The Beardies (mostly ex Wychwood customers). His sermons were clear, following him would guarantee immortality. Sadly for his subscribers he then promptly died.

Refuge

One of the most iconic buildings in Manchester is Refuge Assurance on Oxford Rd. Once part of the sensational quartet on the corner of Whitworth St with The Palace Theatre, The Cornerhouse and The Continental 2.

The Conti had the world's first submerged dancefloor. The sight of the word REFUGE spelt out in huge letters has long brought comfort to travellers arriving back at Oxford Rd after a diabolical camping holiday somewhere in the wilds.

The original building was finished in 1895 by the legend Alfred Waterhouse and the spectacular 217ft clock tower with the worker bee logo, was added after his death, by his architect son Paul. Mrs Pankhurst's statue is situated just down the road from The Refuge. She would have frowned on the practices of the Dukinfield Insurance giant. Women working in the typing pool would have to re-apply for their job if they dared to get married. Waterhouse's legacy in Manchester is fantastic, from that odd shaped Town Hall to the good-looking bits of Manchester University and this architectural masterpiece. So, who to thank for this Victorian grandeur? Alf was a Quaker from the posh bit of Liverpool. Aigburth. So posh it even has a cricket pitch. Cricket playing scousers is just wrong. The Refuge will soon mark the northern tip of the 'University Corridor' just closer to the city centre than the criminally named Circle Square. Let's hope the old gem never gets swamped by hideous bland skyscrapers. Relatively recently the building has been taken on by Principle Hotels with catering provided by DJs turned foodies Luke Cowdrey and Justin Crawford (Unabombers). They are the men behind the exceptional Volta (Didsbury).

Walking into the hotel, the first thing you see is the spectacular glass dome acquired from an unknown Scottish railway station. Wow.

Do all Scottish train stations look like this? The wonderful marble and brass staircase has been restored to its full glory and thankfully for any visiting typists is no longer Gentlemen Only. The humbler staircase at the back of the building is said to be haunted by the ghost of a heartbroken war widow who threw herself down it a century or so ago.

Guidebooks still reference the gorgeous interior tiling of Burmantoft faience. Which part of the world do these exotic creations come from? North Africa, Greece, Rome? No. Yorkshire! Burmantoft may well have been fine once, but now it is one of Leeds's less salubrious high-rise hell holes.

In the 1960s, Hammer Films shot 'gritty northern drama' "Hell is a City" in Manchester. The fight scenes were filmed on top of The Refuge, with glimpses of The Palace Theatre and Oxford Rd Station. Billie Whitelaw played a moll, Donald Pleasance a bookie, and Stanley Baker played himself as a surly anti-hero, or Welshman. Our city godfathers were horrified as it painted Manchester in such a bad light. They were long gone when Shameless came along.

Some gloriously hip people in the Refuge by Volta bar this afternoon, chatting about fabrics. Judging by the speed they were sipping their drinks though, don't think any of them ever made into another of the buildings previous incarnations. Copperface Jacks once occupied the downstairs space on the corner across from The Palace. It still exists, anonymously and only used for special occasions maybe if the Unabombers wanted to play some tunes. In the old days it was seriously frowned upon to even look sober in here.

On a mission today to source one of their world-famous Manchester Kebabs but mistakenly ventured into the swish restaurant. An observant member of staff who looked not unlike a Unabomber must have thought "That looks like a bloke who has had a kebab or two" spotted my error and guided me back to the bar area. It is here that kebab is king.

Yorkshire pudding wrap, crispy lamb shawarma, pickled slaw, Vimto sriracha and sweet chilli sauce teamed with a bottle of First Chop Pale Ale (Eccles). Legendary lunch.

Royal Northern College of Music

In 1893 Charles Halle founded the Royal Manchester College of Music. 80 years later it merged with the Northern School of Music and set up home on Oxford Rd as what we now know as the RNCM. The lovely building is an opulent place for a gig. A top venue with fantastic pure acoustics and that crucial extra comfortable seating.

This is much appreciated by tonight's more mature crowd. These are people who if they were flicking through the channels and found Antiques Roadshow, they would actually watch it.

Back home in the States, Gretchen Peters is a huge star. The multi award winning singer songwriter has no doubt tread less posh boards than these making her way up the Nashville ladder. Her beautiful crystal-clear voice holds the crowd rapt from the opening bars. Husband Barry Walsh is a member of the fine band and talented support act Kim Richey adds more stunning vocals. Gretchen can somehow fit a full life story into just a few verses. What a skill. Sad lives and injustice are a speciality. Melancholia laced with optimism. Even the tale of her late mother coming to her in a dream with the line "There is a love that makes a cup of tea" should sound like a maudlin Mrs Doyle but coming from Gretchen you can feel the hurt but also the hope.

Mostly her observations are spot on apart from one that flies miles off target "I know a lot of you were thinking of going to Ed Sheeran tonight" No we weren't. It had been a sweltering day and Gretchen had been out studying the locals "Manchester! What happened to the weather? I've seen lots of very pale people stumbling about blinking their eyes, looking up at the sky, like they've just come out of a cave"

At an earlier leg of the tour in Newcastle she had met an adoring fan at the merch stall post gig who was buying the latest album "Gretchen I loved the last two albums but they seem so sad" Melancholic Gretchen "Dude, you haven't quite worked this out yet"

A campaigner for justice and a supporter of the oppressed she cannot hide her dismay and disgust at the result of the last US election. Shaking her head bewildered "I really don't know. Just love each other more than they can hate"

To everyone's delight she segues two huge crowd favourites "Bus to St Cloud" and (the greatest song ever about having a sly fag) "Five minutes" together. Then to get the thought of Trump completely out of her hair they play a hard rocking encore. Huge ovation. Accomplished stuff

You know that feeling when you are about to meet a hero. Will they live up to expectations? What can you ask them that is original? Merch stalls are always entertaining especially when manned by the band themselves. The teenybopper in everyone seems to take over. At the end of a Charles Watson gig at Soup Kitchen I queued to buy his CD behind a couple of his most ardent fans who both had the t-shirts and huge beaming smiles. As they got closer, they were almost hyperventilating, excitement growing, egging each other on. They had wanted to ask him forever about an incident at an old Slow Club gig in Sheffield. Suddenly, they were thrust to the front. Brain freeze. She floundered "Charles err" He struggled to take over "When err. Where did you get that shirt from?" Charles "Charity shop in Dorking" That was it, chance gone, more t-shirts bought, and they were off. Maybe next time.

Top Tunes "Five minutes" Gretchen Peters "You've got your way of leaving "Charles Watson

Sale; Robert Bolt

Despite its peaceful canal side walks and leafy surrounds there always seems to be something incendiary about Sale. If a group of bomb disposal experts went for a night out in the town, they would be nervous as hell.

Just out of the town centre though at 131 Northenden Rd is a blue plaque to an ex resident, the brilliant playwright and screenwriter, Robert Bolt. Former Manchester Grammar School pupil Robert won an Academy award for the screenplay for the film version of his own play, A Man for all Seasons, and also for the hugely popular, Dr Zhivago. He also received numerous awards for Lawrence of Arabia, and his adaption of Madame Bovary. Robert never tried to claim any writing credits for John Mills' Oscar in Ryan's Daughter as John played a mute village idiot. This film also starred Robert's wife, the slightly zany, Sarah Miles. Robert these days would be perceived as extreme left wing having once been jailed for his opposition to nuclear arms proliferation in 1961. Seductive Sarah was truly the love of his life, so much so that he was married to her twice, 1967-75 and

1988 up until his death in 1995. In keeping with their eccentric relationship, after a huge champagne wake, Sarah buried Robert in an eco-friendly cardboard coffin in the back garden under the croquet lawn. (urban foxes weren't such a problem back then) He was dressed in a huge scarlet gown and pink scarf. A little like graduating from MGS.

Some people believe Sarah and Robert were responsible for an acting tradition that still survives today. The non-contact mwah mwah luvvie's kiss. One of Sarah's quotes is "Drinking your own urine is wonderful for the skin" Over breakfast 'You look radiant today darling, do you want any juice with that?" "No thanks I've made my own"

Service Included

In the factory where I work the machinery can prioritise who it provides ingredients for. It will fulfil requests from the bottom of the queue if it recognises them as being from someone more important. Some orders it immediately flags as being of less importance.

Much the same principle is applied by Koffee Pot, the purveyor of a fine full Irish (i.e. includes white pudding) on Oldham St. Since its move from Stevenson Sq. its axis seems even further tilted towards the hipster population. It does retain much of its shambolic charm though, through the delightfully distracted serving staff.

On a previous visit I had found this hilarious when an overly loud party of American tourists couldn't get their fill of maple syrup pancakes.

Every time the charming waitress walked away from the whinging, the matriarch uttered "How rude".

Although a genuine hipster can automatically sense another (like paratroopers) there are still some basic ground rules that must be followed.

For Henry: cycling helmet (no bike), beard, three quarter length skinny jeans, no socks, already on your mobile and laptop at the ready "The usual sir?" "Yes, vegan bran flakes, organic honey and soya milk please" For Henrietta: as above minus beard, but add something lacy or a funky hat, some piercings, handbag with fringe, and a score of bracelets. Footwear seems to be important in the hierarchy. Converse all-star hi black canvass basketball boots or a pair of Dolly Parton's suede cowboy boots with tassels gets express service. I was still waiting, and all of these had been and gone.

Eventually I managed to get my top of the free-range fry up after pleading "How do you get served in here?" Sympathetic smile from behind the counter she recognised someone who'd never seen Flight of the Conchords. I only usually read the price on the bill but when I spotted rose tea, was fairly confident it wasn't mine. Think the staff trainer was away in Laos. Beguiled or brow beaten I still left a tip. Love this place and they have free music papers.

Talking of fringed handbags, my sister's friend Anne once turned up with a very impressive number. She had been in Istanbul and a market trainer had cornered her. 'Give me the brand and style you like, and I can make you an exact copy" Unfortunately by the time she got back to Manchester the P had fallen off and she was walking around with a rada handbag Sometimes there is a genuine language barrier between civvies and hipsters. One Sunday morning on my way to work I had to get off the tram in Chorlton as I was famished. Luckily the trendy Post Office Cafe was open.

Result. Hungrily I shouted my order "Two bacon barms please" Only to be greeted with the kind of look usually reserved for when Gillian McKeith makes an order.

The two servers looked aghast "What did he say?" The awkwardness was a broken by a grittier voice of reason from the kitchen "Tomato bread alright?" Barm cakes are not welcome in Chorlton.

My favourite shopping crisis in Chorlton happened in Morrisons. A very well to do mum charging down an aisle with kids in tow repeating "Stilton, Stilton, Stilton" Just a couple of miles south at Wythenshawe Civic Centre the locals charge down the aisle chanting "Fosters, Fosters, Fosters"

Seville

You can't beat that special relationship that builds between lifelong neighbours such as Spain and Portugal. In Seville for a match I found out that one of the funniest words in the Spanish language at the moment is Mourinho. Picked up by an ebullient taxi driver, the first thing he said was "Manchester? Ah Mourinho. The Special One" and dissolved into giggles. They even know the expression 'Park the bus'.

A dire 0-0 ground on late into the warm Spanish night. With no direct flights from Manchester, people just stood around chatting about the roundabout journeys they'd made to get here and ignored the game. I stood next to a bloke who had travelled via Gibraltar and was impressed by his Manc mannerisms and Shaun Ryder accent. I told him watching Mourinho's football was a bit like seeing a dog with a popped ball in its mouth. It's mine I'll do what I want with it. He seemed to relax after that, and I found out he was Mark from Matlock (Spa Reds) and he was a headmaster! Image is everything.

The next day with no football to worry about was far more laid back. 22 degrees in February, not a cloud in the sky. Early morning in the Old Town I was looking up at an impressive church steeple and saw the unmistakeable shadow of an Alsatian trotting along a ledge three floors up. As I crossed the road to get a better look, three cleaning ladies emerged from the building opposite waving tea towels and shouting in Spanish "Go back Go back" I think they were talking to the dog. Just caught a glimpse of him, huge smile on his face before he hopped back off the ledge to safety. Big relief to the four of us, he was just having a lark in the sun.

After getting my breath back, I took a moment and the next thing I saw was the world's angriest nun sweeping into a shop. She was having a key cut. Which one of the sisters had lost the key and where was it to? Match eclipsed already; this couldn't be a bad day.

Found wandering around St Catalina and another church hungry work. Absolutely starving so couldn't walk past Los Claveles restaurant. The interior was great to look at, walls covered with religious imagery, wonderful tiling and impressive hanging jambons. Could spend an hour or two in here. Two smartly dressed easy going barmen, one of whom immediately brought over an English menu. I avoided the painful sounding 'Ground shrimp and cuttlefish balls' and chose Iberica Stew (braised pork cheek) and it was lovely. I was soon joined by a couple from Guingamp in Brittany.

Barman Rubio immediately brought over an Italian menu and seemed offended he had Italians in. The couple asked to borrow my English menu and seemed offended he thought they were Italian. Near neighbour squabbling again. The woman later insisted on sharing her plate of olives with me and the three of us settled in to watch the shenanigans. Turned out Rubio was far less relaxed without his sidekick. When numero uno went outside to fix a scooter with some local lads, Rubio's blood pressure went through the ornate roof. Very much to the amusement of my Guingamp friends. Glasses crashed into the sink, menus were scattered, and orders forgotten. Mayhem. They stayed through the late morning period (old boys reading the paper) through the chaotic ladies who lunch (the decibel level soared) and into the let's have a swift half before the school run gang. Great entertainment.

Calm was restored when scooter fanatic returned and after a jovial couple of hours my French friends moved on. I shouted "God bless Gwingamp" after them. Madame looked horrified but the husband came back laughing and said closing his finger and thumb together as if to say much shorter "Gangam Gangam" Rubio had stirred their nationalism. In the city of Carmen and Don Juan these Andalusians have got things just right. They really know how to enjoy themselves. One of the bar regulars Rafa still texts me "How is the Special One?" I did have a good look but strangely couldn't find a barbers called Figaro.

Refreshed after the obligatory siesta I made it into Viniato (Guevara and Lynch) a celebration of Cuban and Irish culture! Extensive menu but had the local speciality and one with the longest name Quesadilos de pringa casero con queso cheddar, beros y salsa cruder. Didn't bother trying to say it simply pointed at it on the menu.

Carrying on toward town passed the towering wooden mushroom parasol designed to shelter the shopping centre from the heat. It should be visible from the moon, but I hadn't been able to spot it last night after a deluge of Cruzcampo. Victoria Eugenia, apart from its sun-drenched terrace reminds me of a Manchester bar. The staff are hilarious. I gave the barmaid Angellina the Sevilla v Manchester wristband you were supposed to wear to gain entry to the ground the previous night. She put it on like it was made by Faberge "Ah Sevilla is always beautiful. Manchester err? I don't know Manchester".

Using the when in Rome (sorry Rubio) policy I simply copied what the locals were ordering. Coffee then scrambled egg mushrooms and prawns, a Larios gin and tonic and finally a super dry Solear sherry. Angellina was concerned I got the right sherry, so she gave me a taster of the sweet and my fillings fell out. Another barman started his shift. Apron on immediately and worded up by the others over he came "My friend, Manchester eh? You love The Beatles yeah? Paul McCartney!" Puzzled look and turned away then turned back round laughing. Genuine wind up merchants.

Still not finished, as the evening wore on and the bar got busier, the boss arrived. After a brief team talk to the staff, he wandered over to chat football. Aside from Angellina everybody else in here was a fan of the other local side Betis. We all agreed on a huge dislike for the Spanish super clubs Real and Barca. A while later a lad walked in a Barca hat, the boss feigned horror and shouted in jovial fashion "Hey hey amigo no Barca" then turned pointed at me and said "Him Mourinho auto bus".

Great city.

Simone Felice

Leaf on Portland St behind that unpromising entrance is a bit of a gem. Those breakfasts! A real class joint and the downstairs venue is almost decadently opulent for central Manchester. Arriving late and stumbling through the wrong gap in the curtains was horrified to find I was one of the last punters in. Simone was already on stage and the hushed capacity crowd had long taken their seats. Self-consciously I made my way to the back in the striking church like silence. The reverential hush was maintained throughout as the crowd listened intently to Simone's poetic songs of lovers and losers, rejection and despair! For many it seemed an almost hallucinatory experience. His devoted fans had been on a long journey with their hero. This was a long-term relationship from his time with the family band The Felice Brothers, his soulful spin off The Duke and The King, a momentary lapse into a Mumford and Sons collaboration, through to his solo albums.

There is something about those who have cheated death that seems to engender a healthy creative streak. Simone hasn't messed around, dodging the grim reaper twice. An aneurism at the age of 12 had left him clinically dead for several minutes. If that wasn't bad enough, just over a decade ago a health check revealed his heart was operating at only 12% of its capacity, and his doctor told him "There is no medical reason you are still alive" Double creative streak.

Haunting lyrics on the likes of "Angel by my side" which sadly for the rest of us (from a man in the know) states that he has seen too much to believe in an afterlife. He also sings of happily welcoming the apocalypse if it meant he could start all over with his true love. Simone's only novel Black Jesus is the jolly tale of an army veteran falling for a 'busted angel' It can be bleak where he was brought up in New York State's Catskill Mountains.

Two forty-minute sets flew by. Highlights were the pitch perfect and ultra-respectful singalongs firstly to "The morning I get to hell" "My only happy song. It's about the passing of my grandad" Then right at the end Simone still perched on his stool conducted a choirlike rendition of "Bye bye Palenville" Finally he climbed off that stool for a bow and a little dance to the closing music of "The End" by The Doors. Magnificent melancholy masterpiece of a gig.

An almost Moses like parting of the crowds as he made his way to sign some merch. Apart from a very few, those satiated devoted souls seemed to dissolve quickly into the ether. I was left virtually alone at the downstairs bar having a nightcap. Out of nowhere the great man appeared. No 'Whiskey in my whiskey' as he had once sung in the Felice Brothers. After the heart problems Simone sticks to carrot juice or ginger tea. He describes himself as the least likely rock star you will ever meet. Sometimes you can stumble across him doing a Native American chant back home in a Catskill's forest.

Arriving less spectrally two groupies appeared, a mother and daughter from Oldham. They hadn't been able to find a pen but needed that album signing. SF had once said "I've always been

walking that stone wall between this world and the other"
Nothing quite so deep this time but even "Have you got a pen?"
sounded mystical to me. Checking the pocket was relieved to find
one for a change that didn't have Fred Done's name on it. Hoping
for a Parker instead it was a bright yellow gaudy thing. I handed it
to groupie mum who looked at it and handed it to my new mate Si
who also read it, signed the album and rolled it back along the
bar. I looked hoping the biro was inscribed with something trendy
like Extinction Rebel, instead it was "Cat's Protection 90th
Anniversary" Maybe the man from the mountains approved.
Top Tunes: Simone Felice "You and I belong" "Courtney Love"
Whenever you meet someone famous their every word sticks with
you. Five days before the 1999 Champions League final we were
making our way to Spain. All alone at the bar in Terminal 2 at
Manchester Airport in amongst all the United bunting stood a
grim-faced Howard Kendall "Hey Howard where you flying to?"
"Anywhere to get away from this" as some tiny red and white
flags fluttered around his head.
In ancient times if you ever bumped into a footballer out
socialising it was more than likely to be a goalkeeper. It was a
tradition even up to professional level to have 10 footballers and
then one nutcase keeper, usually the one who used to do the
football card in the pub vault. Every team searched for that
special one. United had Roche. Then there was Sprake (Leeds)
Lawrence (Liverpool) Burridge (Anybody) and McRae, Corrigan,
Dibble, Weaver and Nixon (Man City) The Brazilian national
team took this to another level by taking no goalkeepers to the
World Cup and just playing a waiter from their hotel between the
sticks. I once had the pleasure of meeting the legendary Eric
Nixon in the even more legendary Manor House in Didsbury and
remember his words to this day "Oi You've forgot your change"

Smokehouse

Sadly often by the time you get to a restaurant that has had rave
reviews it is long gone. Such a difficult market and they cannot
survive on goodwill alone. After glowing recommendations was
pasta excited to make it to Buca di Pizza on Lloyd St in between
The Nags and the Gentleman's club. Unfortunately, the bailiffs

had beat me to it. Great pizza allegedly but an even greater gas bill.

Next door at Smokehouse, the New Yorker pizza featuring nearly a full brisket more than made up for it. Just three diners this Thursday afternoon but the lovely waitress explained it away as "Well we are so hidden away here and underground" Down these stairs at one time was either Deville's or its sister bar Lazy Lil's I couldn't quite make out the geography.

Deville's was always a bit left field, avant garde or as they said in Wythenshawe 'full of weirdos' Its sister bar Lil's was far more down to earth which is where most of the patrons ended up after deciding a go on the bucking bronco was a good idea after a couple of Grolsch. What kudos you got if you made it into Deville's with a bandaged wrist or cut head after a flying dismount from the angry bull. Special praise was reserved for those who had projectile vomited over their mates from the mechanical monster. Heady intoxicating days long before health and safety took all the bulls into care. The waitress explained that huge changes were afoot. The new Le Corbusier, Sir Gary Neville was to personally pedestrianise the whole area including Bootle and Lloyd St to create a huge European style stroll zone around the town hall. Sadly, Lord Burnham's seat is not due to re-open until 2024. Seems we have employed the same family of Spanish builders who have been working on La Sagrada Familia in Barcelona for a century or so.

Soccer Mommy

It's just over 15 years since Sophie Allison aka Soccer Mommy penned her first song "What the heck is a cowgirl?" at the age of 5. Sadly, she doesn't include this one in her set tonight at Deaf Institute. For a Kelly Clarkson fanatic Sophie's tunes have a startling brooding intensity. I presume like many artists she deals with her own self-doubt by singing about it. Ominous undercurrents abound. Hopefully her relationship advisory blockbuster "Your dog" is just a feminist anthem rather than a warning to boyfriend Julien who plays alongside her in the band. Mind you on YouTube the most complimentary review of Julien says "Who the hell is that guy on guitar, he ruins the whole thing".

She has crammed a lot into these 21 years, including touring with one of her heroes, the positively ancient 24-year-old Phoebe Bridgers. She is preaching to the converted here. An adoring sell-out crowd. The simple arrangements and powerful lyrics about the plight of the outsider really resonate with so many. Her sparse version of Springsteen's "I'm on fire" is played to a complete hush. World at her feet? Somehow you can't see someone with a first album called "Songs for the recently sad" going down the Kelly Clarkson route. Where will the next 15 years take her? Should be fascinating to watch.

Top Tune: "Scorpio Rising" Soccer Mommy

Snapped Ankles

It was only a couple of weeks after my last visit that me and my friend A were back in Koffee Pot. Just can't stay away. This time we were on a mission to get a copy of music magazine, Loud and Quiet, which had an article on local legends, DUDS. Exclusively the band are all past or present Peveril staff, or at least customers. Criminally they still haven't found a place for the pub's top musician, landlord Maurice.

A very quiet evening in KP, just two women sat at a table near the bar. As we approached, I heard A utter "Oh my God" What had disturbed her so much? They had soft drinks and were playing Lego. This is totally unacceptable even for the Northern Quarter. Please keep this kind of behaviour behind closed doors.

The band we were heading to see tonight were Snapped Ankles. They are part of the musical community that has sprung up in Stoke Newington. A kind of boho version of Hackney. They come dressed as forest creatures or trees and you really hope that a Rees-Mogg isn't hiding under all that foliage. Some difficulties they face are passing dogs when they nip out for a pre gig fag and a bizarre incident at Green Man's, Nature Nurture woodland stage when something tried to come home to roost. Driving guitars, Krautrock, and delirious synth pop dance tunes are where they are at. Part punk part Ground Force. The fantastic homemade log synths would have got the thumbs up from Tommy Walsh and Titchmarsh.

169

At times some of the vocals were less clear than Mark E Smith gargling but this was all about them incessant thumping beats. They laid down a challenge to even the most reluctant of dancers. After absolutely killing it at Salford's 'Sounds of the other City' festival, they seem to have imported many new friends from down Chapel St. A raucous and happy crowd, though A was taking some convincing. "I just can't take them seriously dressed like that" I could see her point. What if the BBC announcer said "Newsnight tonight with Emily Maitlis" and she came on dressed like a small copse? A was soon won round. Glorious must-see band 9/10

Top Tunes "I want my minute's back" "Hanging with the moon" Snapped Ankles

Sometime later we were lucky to see Snapped Ankles again at the opening of Fairfield Social Club, on Temperance St. I love the fact that like something out of Sin City there are now 3 breweries on Temperance St. A great new live venue and irresistible Manchester Union Lager on tap. Another storming gig by the band and at the end with forensic detective work we managed to recognise singer Paddy by his chunky watch. He signed an album and even did a little sketch of the woodland synths on the cover. Cornered under an avalanche of questions he buckled and revealed they would probably keep the creatures of the forest image for good. As we were leaving, I said to A "You know he thinks were barking, and he spends his days dressed as a bush" See you at Psych fest Paddy unless you've changed your watch.

The Soft Cavalry

In 2014 Steve Clarke by his own admission was at a very low point. A recent bitter divorce and a bit part in a Ricky Gervais film had done nothing to improve his mood or sense of humour. These were hard times and a creative low in his life. The ex-Dumdums bassist was now making a living as a jobbing musician and sometime road manager. It was in this role that he first set eyes on Rachel Goswell of Slowdive as he tried to cram his own and the band's equipment into the tour van. Steve remembers he was sporting a full-on rock n roll hangover at the time, but it was love at first sight. In his words "She turned my world upside down" The confidence and support she provides has meant he has now achieved his ultimate if previous tentative ambition to front his own band. Speaking of the recovery from the bad times Steve says "With the right people around you, you get through and find a level of hope"

The couple married in 2018 and moved to the rock n roll hotbed of Devon where most of the songs on the debut album were written and vocals recorded.

Tonight's gig had been moved from the sparkly Pink Room upstairs, to the murky basement. When support act Death by Stampede played, only a handful of gig goers had taken their places in the venue. As he stood at the bar later his mate said to him "You looked like a ghost performing to five lost souls"

The crowd had swelled to around 30 by the time The Soft Cavalry sauntered cheerfully on stage. The meagre turn out can easily be explained by the fact it was only their second gig and the official album release was still two days away. This prompted Steve to say, "You may only know the two tracks" Somewhere in the darkness a voice said "Maybe three" but I think that might have been the drummer.

Rachel lit up the gloom in mega sparkly top and greeted the throng with "Hello. Wow this is a very select crowd" The onstage chemistry was clear from the very start. Steve's jovial but not encouraging first line of "Hey. Let's soft rock" brought a smile from his wife. Two chords later she called an early time-out due to perceived technical problems. This brought a return smile and look of bemusement from Steve "Did you have a good sleep this afternoon while I was setting up here?"

These songs are a real labour of love and a very personal tribute to Rachel. Set somewhere between shoegaze and synthpop, Steve had long ago exhausted his love for guitar music during his time as a Dumdum. Rachel, soulmate, keyboards, vocals and spiritual guide also admits to being her beloved's lyric editor "You should cut that verse out, it's rubbish" What a lovely devoted couple. Managed to speak to them later in the bar and apologised for the crowd being smaller than an Archie's queue. Steve was still just high on life "No matter we loved it. And anyway, everyone is still making their way back from Glastonbury" A genuine musical love story that hopefully runs and runs. Was it Robbie Williams who once said "If music be the love of food..."

Top Tunes: The Soft Cavalry "Bulletproof" "Dive" Dumdums "Army of Two"

Stalybridge

In America people talk of escaping from Dodge City as finding a way out of a desperate place or situation. In Tameside its easy, from Platform 1 Stalybridge station just hop on the train back to Manchester. The old cowtown next to Cottonopolis was once quite rightly described as "a disorganised village of lawlessness" Any place that had a nightclub called Rififi (rough translation: mass brawl) as recently as 2013, knows its local clientele. You could sip a Flaming Lamborghini inside while looking at one outside in the car park. How did Michael Portillo, clad in yellow blazer and pink strides, survive these mean streets when he turfed up to film the famous buffet bar for his series, Great British Railway Journeys? The town itself has a fascinating history. In the beautiful scenery high above the unsettled yokels, once stood the top-ranking hill fort, Buckton Castle, a refuge for Ranulf, the second Earl of Chester, from his marauding enemy Peveril. It was in these hills that botanist John Bradbury honed his skills. A mill worker by day and flora/fauna genius and lecturer at night and on his occasional day off.

John is far better known in Las Vegas than Staley Vegas as he went on to map much of the interior of the US after securing funding from the Liverpool Botanic Gardens. His remit was to study cotton plants and improve the supply and quality of imports to the UK. One of the first men to travel the American badlands, his tough Stalybridge background helped him to survive where many of his fellow explorers fell victim to starvation, cliffs or rapids.

One of John's pupils was the man with the most Tameside name of all time, Jethro Tinker. Jeth was so enamoured by the beauty of the Pennine town that he never left and spent all his 83 years here. A huge flora and fauna enthusiast he was known to walk to Buxton and back just to collect a particular specimen. His blue plaque stands at the entrance to Stalybridge Country Park.

Stalybridge has also contributed to popular culture. Staffordshire fish monger Jack Judge (probably a stage name) was a winner of an early Britain's got Talent and wrote the smash-hit 'It's a long way to Tipperary' in the town during a boozy Christmas night out. It was first performed at the Stalybridge Hippodrome on New Year's Eve 1912. The streets of the town haven't changed that much over the years so much so that John Schlesinger filmed part of his WW2 film 'Yanks' here without resorting to fake scenery or props.

More importantly to some, Methodist preacher and defender of the working class, Joseph Rayner Stephens (1805-79) was from Stalybridge. He campaigned against the Poor Law of 1834 and the working hours for children of 5am to 8pm. Childcare wasn't necessary back then. He supported the implementation of the People's Charter arguing for the vote, a reasonable wage and a secure life for all, not just the aristocracy. His insistence that workhouses were simply 'prisons for the poor' led to his own imprisonment.

His words were often quoted by supporters of the General Strike in 1842. Stalybridge was the epicentre of the strike and here it was known as The Plug Riots. Jeremiah Lees a local mill owner had proposed a 25% pay cut for his workers. Strikers removed the plugs from the factory boilers rendering them useless. They gathered support from all over Tameside and up to twenty thousand marched to Manchester behind the banner "The men of Stalybridge will follow wherever danger points the way"

Later that century the mill workers were to put themselves through great personal suffering in aid of another just cause. The American Civil War had caused a shortage of the cotton that kept the mills working.

Sadly, some unscrupulous bosses and early futures traders were guilty of stockpiling forcing up the price of the finished clothing. The ordinary man in the mill was not so lucky. Over 7000 were laid off in Stalybridge alone. Only 5 out of 39 local factories were in production. Food vouchers were issued and soup kitchens and beggars on the streets were commonplace. In a show of international solidarity though, the mill workers pledged support to Abe Lincoln's blockade of the southern ports of the US which prevented the export of cotton picked by slaves. Marx spoke of the indirect slavery of the working man of England and the direct slavery of the black man across the Atlantic.

Mayor Abel Heywood promised solidarity with the cotton pickers and championed equality in a speech at the Free Trade Hall. President Lincoln personally thanked the working people of Manchester for their "sublime Christian heroism" A time of great hardship, amazingly the US sent aid ships to the strikers of Lancashire that even the Confederate flag flying dockers at Liverpool agreed to unload for free. Liverpool despite being a major player in international slave trade was keen not to rock the boat and maintain its place as an international port. Poor Abe L was assassinated before the abolition of slavery in 1865 and a much-changed cotton industry was able to make a comeback.

In 1863 the Riot Act was read as civil unrest erupted in Stalybridge. Why was aid for the poor coming from outside sources and not the affluent mill owners? Authorities mobilised the Hussars to quell the violence.

In a bizarre twist, a known political agitator and very Irish sounding rabble rouser named Murphy arrived in Stalybridge and blamed the unrest on Irish immigrants (In times of trouble scapegoat immigrants. Who would have thought it?) He called for local Catholic priests to be hung from trees! Thankfully the locals pulled the plug before the Murphy Riots escalated.

The most famous celebrity couple from Stalybridge are Gibbon and Hannah Mitchell. It was a one-off Christian name. He didn't come from a long line of gibbons. Gib was a founder of the Independent Labour Party with Keir Hardie and an ardent socialist. His wife Hannah was a member of the WSPU (Women's Social and Political Union) A contemporary though not a huge fan of the Pankhursts she objected to their authoritarian nature and unilateral decision making. Hannah also revealed Gibbon's attitude to household chores and said, "He might be a socialist but he's certainly not a feminist" The cheeky monkey. Hannah became a prominent member of Manchester City Council despite having the sum total of two weeks formal education. A tradition continued to this day.

Back to that train station which was formally opened in 1845 after criticism that transport times in the Northern Powerhouse were slow. A canal journey from Manchester to Sheffield was taking up to 8 days. The fantastic buffet bar was added in 1885 and has survived regally over the years.

Stock full of railway memorabilia, you can order a pint of real ale watched over by the image of Queen Victoria etched into the mirror above the fire. The steak and ale pies are a thing of beauty that will make you pledge to return for more. In the 1990s the buffet bar was saved by campaigning locals when it was suggested it needed updating into a Traveller's Fare with Ginsters pasties.

Easier to agree with these locals when you don't have the Hussars to call on.

Steve Mason

It's great to hear some real friendly banter from band to crowd, especially if you can understand it. Steve Mason, once of the brilliant Beta Band went from battling the huge hype of Blur and Oasis to taking on Blair and Bush. The Beta's themselves were great and any band with a member called Lone Pigeon and a penchant for self-destruction can't be bad. Steve definitely used to make his voice heard but battling his own demons as well led him to escape from the world to a "forest in Fife"

Joyously 2016 saw him back with the aptly named 'Meet the Humans' and a sell out Sunday night at Academy 2. About as far removed from a forest as you could get. Humbled and overjoyed by the turnout, Steve had great craic with the many Scots who had travelled down. The more at ease he felt the more his accent veered toward Rab C Nesbitt after 10 Buckfasts, leaving most of the locals baffled. Steve did get at least one pint as he appeared in Big Hands later still beaming. Top guy, top gig.

The problem of how much to converse with the crowd will always be there. The brilliant J Mascis (Dinosaur Jnr) once did a full gig at Ruby Lounge sat on a stool centre stage without even saying hello. J was letting his guitar do the talking but from the back of the hall all you could see was the top of his baseball cap. It was like listening to the radio through your neighbour's kitchen window.

He could have the right idea though to limit the idle chatter. The wonderful Haley Bonar was gasping for air in sweltering conditions in Night and Day. Searching for a bottle of water she asked "Hello Night and Day. Any questions?" Awkward silence then "Did your trousers shrink in the wash?" Perplexed but still smiling "The Manchester weather did that. Any more questions?" More shuffling feet "What did you have for lunch?" Not since the days of Peter Powell has there been a worse music interview. Haley escaped lightly compared to Joan Wasser (Joan as Policewoman) who had the misfortune to have an Inverdale in the audience. Unimpressed by Gorilla's air conditioning she needed a time out "It's so hot in here. Anybody got any questions?" Inverdale "How hot is it in that jumpsuit?"

Celebrity audience members can also cop for it. A slightly smug looking Tim Farron (Now a Z- celeb) trying to look cool at an Avalanches gig was hit with the low blow "Off to the village tonight Tim?"

Top Tunes "To a door" Steve Mason "Dry the Rain "Beta Band "Lost War" Haley Bonar "Is it Done "J Mascis

Stockport; Where every moon is a full one

There aren't many bands with a link to Stockport otherwise you'd end up constantly banging your head on road signs. 'Stockport Home of Blossoms' on every point of entry seems a bit ungracious to past entertainment greats like Mike Yarwood who got zilch civic recognition.

Many people think that David Lynch visited Stockport before writing Twin Peaks. I once went in McDonalds in the town centre at 7.30 am on a Sunday morning and I'm sure the X-Files music was playing. Engels was an expert on the state of the working class, and he declared Stockport to be "excessively repellent" and "a smoky hole" He never did get that job as a town estate agent.

My mother's friend always said Stopfordians were all driven mad by inhaling the glue fumes in the local hat factories. She would then emphasise the point by saying "and they are all inbred as well" In mythology Hercules's 13th labour was to drive the Offerton Circular bus for a full weekend with Stockport people getting on and off at each stop. Immensely cruel it proved to be his demise.

Paul Morley might still be the most famous person ever from Stockport along with local polo shirt manufacturer Fred Perry. There was also Sabrina (Norma Ann Sykes) the 1950's glamour model who was the poster girl for the original St Trinians film. Sabrina eventually emigrated to America where her assets led to her being used in one film as a stand in for Jayne Mansfield. As Eric Morley (no relation) used to say, her vital statistics were 41-19-36. Norma was from Heaviley.

One little known fact about Stockport is that back in the 1173 it had its own timber motte and bailey castle. In the 13th Century it was replaced by a more practical stone one. There was a famous battle here when Geoffrey de Costentyn held off an attack by Henry II. The castle was owned by the Warren family who used it mostly as a jail as they preferred to live in Poynton Manor. George Warren eventually knocked the castle down in 1775 for development. A cotton mill was built on the site. Some say though that under a parking meter on Mealhouse Brow there is one single surviving castle stone.

Top Stockport Tune: "The Dean and I" 10cc Not Eric Stewart's favourite song but has the great first line "Hey kids let me tell you where I met your ma" The answer was always The Plaza. 10cc vocalist Lol Creme went on to form the Art of Noise with Paul Morley. Thankfully they were mostly instrumental, so Paul wasn't let loose with the lyric writing. Would hazard a bet though that he had some part in naming one album 'The Seduction of Claude Debussy'

Suburban Chorlton

Having seen a huge thumbs up for Le Tagine, Chorlton on Manchester Confidential, thought what a great place for a Tuesday lunch. When I got there, Google insisted it was open though there was nobody to be seen. I went next door to The Drop having somehow lived a Jerk Chicken free life up to now. It was only after ordering I realised the bloke collecting boxes of veg at the door was Mr Tagine. Who knew that delivery drivers do the same as the Post Office and put a little card through "Have left your cabbages next door" Really enjoyed my West Indian food and the music was amazing in here. Gil Scott Heron, Afroman, Sly and the Family Stone and many more cool tracks I didn't recognise. On the way out asked the ace waitress Miranda what one particular track was "That's the late great William Onyeabor" Nod knowingly, this is Chorlton. She said she had done her own mix for the cafe and thank God, Ed Sheeran didn't exist in her world. In a totally non-Impulse moment Miranda came haring after me when I left "Would you do a review on Trip Advisor? Me and my friends are having a competition to see who gets most likes"

I did a review on TA and ended it with "Great service, soundtrack and food. A little gem" The next review on TA simply said, "No it isn't" Was that from one of Miranda's rivals or someone from Kentucky? Trip Advisor is a harsh platform especially if Americans get near it "Car park was at least 50 yards from the front door"

Not being churlish but some of these Guardian brandishing Chorltonites might never have landed in the Free Trade coffee shops if they knew the origin of the district's name. Chorlton comes from Ceorl = countryman and ton = settlement. Basically Yokelstown.

Chorlton has not always been such a peaceful idyll. As recently as 1835 the local sport was bull baiting! "Watched by hundreds of men of the very lowest character" On the green outside the Horse and Jockey a bull would be tethered, and locals would set their bulldogs on it. Those leafy gutters once ran crimson with blood.

It has though housed its heroes. Sir Arthur Whitten Brown and his mate Johnny Alcock won the fortune of £10 000 in 1919 for the first air crossing of the Atlantic. Born to American parents in Glasgow, Arthur moved to Chorlton when his dad got a job with Westinghouse in Trafford Park. This company built a village for its workforce in the US grid fashion, hence the numbered streets Fifth St etc. A buyout by Metropolitan Carriage Wagon Company and Vickers gave us the legendary Metrovick.

Arthur was an apprentice when war broke out in 1914 and he enlisted with the warriors of the UPS (Universities and Public Schools Brigade) Fearless Arthur took a commission to the Manchester Regiment, and while working in reconnaissance was shot down twice! Did John know this when he hired him to navigate the Vickers Vimy over the Atlantic. Third time lucky. During the record attempt Arthur twice had to climb up above the cockpit to clear snow from the plane's instruments. Then heavy fog meant his sextant was useless, you can imagine that being jettisoned over his shoulder. He still managed to keep the plane flying in almost a straight line. Sixteen hours after leaving Newfoundland they crash landed in a bog in Clifden, Connemara. Mission successful.

A plaque still stands to the legend at his old house at 6 Oswald Rd, Yokelstown.

Support

One of the great joys of gigging is to catch the support band. This could be the biggest gig of their lives and you never know just who you might discover. Slow Readers Club playing on a Saturday afternoon at Blackthorn Festival springs to mind. The crowd thronging the front of the stage were two mums with prams. The kids were off playing in the hay.

A few that have stood out this year. The slightly 'wacky' Mr Ben and The Bens supporting the always entertaining Wave Pictures at Deaf Institute. From way up north in Cumbria with a legion of supporters all in Sunday best (with added bobble hats) determined to blow the roof of the big city. Infectious genuine madness. What do they put in the water in Lancaster?

Afghan Sand Band along with Cabbage are leading Mossley's resurgence from cultural wilderness to a centre of musical excellence. I saw them supporting LA Witch at Soup Kitchen and would struggle to define their sound. Thankfully the Afghan leader Will Owen had already had a go himself "An electronic lexicon of stiff grounded beats and ethereal ascending fog" Will, they don't like that kind of talk up in Mozzley. Best move to Manchester. This was the time that both Winter Hill and Dovestones were tragically ablaze. Mossley could easily have been a wilderness by the time they got home. Interesting band could be the one to watch.

Sad to see the demise of Ruby Lounge and that classical brutalist block. Findlay played the last great gig here in November 2018 and had the support of Sophie and the Giants. A band that just seem to have a certain something. At college when they first practised together, they shocked even themselves with the immediate chemistry. Tonight, it took only one song for ears to prick up, the bar to empty the bar and everyone drift around the corner to watch. True star quality. Will miss the Ruby and its eclectic patrons. Doorman to beard with rucksack "What's in the bag mate?" "It's a jar of organic honey" I carry one everywhere

Susanne Sundfør

With the loss of both Sound Control and Ruby Lounge all new small venues are welcomed with open arms. Peer Hat, Jimmy's, YES are all great venues and the Stoller Hall, part of the Chetham's complex is exceptional. An amazing looking place and wow those comfy seats. I knew it was a different type of crowd when before the gig I saw the bloke in the next seat was heavily embroiled in a hardback book. It was called Royal Flush and wasn't even about poker. Not many of this well-heeled crowd had wandered down Market St with a hotdog pre gig. (Check for mustard stains. How did I get in?))

Norwegian, Susanne Sundfor was the brilliant headline artist tonight and every Scandinavian in the North West seemed to have made the journey. This included two women determined to take in the sites of the new venue stopping twice to take in the classy surrounds and twice tripping up the grumbling queue. All those hours of darkness you'd think they would have spatial awareness. Think I did find some fellow hot dog eaters at the bar at the interval. A Nordic dad let his two daughters into a queue that was already on a tight schedule. Would we get time for a drink at all? Two well spoken, posh suits behind me in the queue moaned loudly but then immediately took stock "Should we have something else then?" "Just get me the biggest bottle... of whatever" I turned around laughing and he said "Do you do that as well? I always end up with Magners It's always the biggest" Interval drinks are essential.

The acoustics in the hall are sensational, definitely the best in Manchester. The piano sounded from another world. The bookworm had been complaining about the overactive air con, pointing to the gaps in the wooden panelling as the source of the draught. I said maybe the builders were from down the road in Cheetham Hill. Now he turned into a heating engineer and went on to explain that it was these gaps that amplified the warm crystal-clear sounds. Though claiming to be Susanne's biggest fan "I've seen her so many times before" he fell asleep not long into the gig only waking to clap after every other song. Had that stunning voice put him into a trance? Were these seats just too comfortable? That book must be rubbish.

Tremendous complex song structures, a bit anarchic. Deep and dark, like one of them Scandi crime thrillers. Somehow the songs never ended up quite where you thought they were going. This would have been a difficult singalong. An absolute treat for Magners drinkers and heating engineers alike and the magical bit was still to come. When Susanne sang 'Undercover' it was near angelic and the crowd were genuinely stunned. Close to perfection. After the finishing note there was silence for a good few seconds as jaws were picked up off the floor. Insanely talented. Standing ovation. Perfect.

Top Tune: "Undercover" Susanne Sundfor (captured on YouTube 'Live at Stoller Hall')

Svanette and The Swiss

In November 2017 United were drawn to play in Basel. Trawling through the 336 possible Air bnbs my attention kept getting drawn back to the same one. Above Svanette's hat shop in Dornach. What an inspired choice, Svanette was a charming lovely host and Dornach was home to Rudolf Steiner's truly fascinating Goetheanum.

I booked very late and we had already bonded over the last-minute emails. Svan "This is a vegan house, will that be OK" Me "Of course, will give it a go" So when I got there late on a Monday night, Svanette (Little Swan) greeted me with some lupin berries for supper. To the unskilled poisonous but prepared by a seasoned vegan, delicious. So much better than a packet of Cheddars.

Breakfast next morning consisted of beetroot hummus on flat bread with watercress and pumpkin, all washed down with a pot of cleansing black tea. Thought my system was holding up well to the health food onslaught until I walked up to the Goetheanum and had to leg it to the Herren.

The Goetheanum must not be missed, a very special and spectacular place. It stands in its own landscaped gardens and is home to the Anthroposophical Society (awareness of humanity) An incredible monumental building constructed between 1925-28 of carved concrete. The astonishing 1000 seat auditorium has a unique spiritual atmosphere. The ceiling paintings and stain glass windows depict images of human evolution. On the 5th floor is Steiner's collaboration with English sculptor Edith Maryon 'The representative of humanity'. My guide Karoline explained its significance and somehow mystically linked it with my life. Unnerving.

During one of our conversations that veered between spirituality to Guinness and back, Little Swan recommended a peaceful walk up the hill to the castle "It will be an easy walk for you. Or you could even get the bus halfway" Thank God for that Swiss stagecoach, the hill was more of a small Alp. The castle was truly stunning. Somehow, I managed to get lost down a housing estate cul de sac searching for the downhill bus stop. Asked a passing local and he was only too pleased to expansively point me in the right direction "Your English is perfect" "Thank you for many years I worked in Plymouth" Surprised I could understand the accent.

Avoided the touristy bars before the game and had a drink with about 20 old local lads in a backstreet boozer. 17.45 they all started getting edgy. 18.00 they were all gone, to beat the curfew. The Swiss rolling pin is still very much in evidence.

A final brilliant breakfast of oat porridge, pomegranate seed and edible flower buds with soya milk. Sensational. Before leaving I even bought a trendy retro flapper hat for my friend Ali. Little Swan recommended a 10-gallon Stetson for me, but I managed to resist. Would look cool on Bern High Street but not so good in The Woodpecker. What a great time, she is a lovely host.

Bought some chocolates in Zurich on the way home. The shop assistant stopped mid-sentence when asking "Alcohol or non-alcohol?" One look at me and she said "Yah ..me too also" At the airport bar nursing a sore head I quietly asked the barman for a small beer. He must yodel on his days off and he shouted back "Why you want a small beer its 6, a large beer is only 7.5" A good point well made.

Watching the departures board, the world suddenly stood still. Men and women looked on entranced. A raven-haired beauty in a striped dress strode through the Terminal. She sure knew how to pull a suitcase. What were the odds she was on the Manchester flight? Huge. But then she smouldered up to our departure gate. Wow. What were the odds she was sat next to me? Vast. Correct. I was sat next to two German Liverpool fans on their way to Anfield and they wanted a singsong. My luck had run out. Love Switzerland.

Goetheanum

Tram stops

There are two tram stops on the Metrolink named after medieval halls. To the south there is Peel Hall, with its six-hundred-year-old bridge and moat. A farmhouse was built on this site around 1810 and only demolished in 1975 when Wythenshawe was sacked by vandals. Just nearby stood the fantastic old inn, The Tudor Tavern, once beloved of Mario Balotelli. The Tudor was always known by locals as The Flying Machine, its original name, hence the confused signwriter.

Way to the east is Clayton Hall, once owned by the Byron family, relatives of the mad, bad, punk poet George Gordon Byron, who was a sort of early John Cooper Clarke. Clayton Hall has also retained its moat, but an overzealous H&S officer decided to drain it and seal it with concrete. Get through that Tony Robinson. The original house was built here for the Clayton family in the 12th century. When Cecilia Clayton married Robert de Byron in 1194 it passed into the hands of the poet's family. The Byrons lived here for over 400 years before flogging the building to the famous Cheetham family, the founders of Chetham's school. Today you can still visit this unique place staffed by lovely enthusiastic volunteers. There is even a small cafe with local delicacies like hot Vimto and sausage rolls. After part of the house was damaged by a sell off to unscrupulous developers, a decision was made to save and remodel the main area in Victorian style. Visitors can dress up in Victorian garb on arrival, or if you are from Droylsden, come as you are.

Sadly in September 2018, The Tudor closed its doors for good, to be replaced by 6 luxury homes. Another vast desert stretching from Sharston to Woodhouse Park without a decent pint in sight. The only place to quench your thirst is the oddly titled Benchill Conservative Club. David Cameron can testify as to what happens to Tories round here.

South Island Son and The Travelling Band

There are some professions that you really wouldn't want to live together en masse less they become too marginalised and radical. Traffic wardens and dental hygienists spring to mind.

Laid back Mancunian music icons The Travelling Band and South Island Son now share a house. Think they will just about get away with it if they remember to name tag the hummus in the fridge and replenish the stock of plectrums and Jack Daniels. Not sure what district they are in, but you can imagine the neighbours banging on the wall shouting, "Think you are in a bloody band or something" Not sure if either "Mopping forwards" or "Passing ships" are signs of the problems of domesticity. Poor Harry Fausting Smith (fiddle) has a bow in both camps, he should live in the attic to avoid arguments.

Glorious low-key Americana from the Souths who are sartorially relaxed in a kind of Debenham's blue cross chic. Great entertainment here, this was all about the music not chasing the filthy lucre. Travelling Band's Jo Dudderidge explained that writing songs about the cynicism of the music industry was a form of therapy then said with a grin "Now the real reason we are here tonight. Check out South Island Son's merch table at the back. They've got some lovely stuff" Some great chat with the crowd including a collective failure to remember the name of a hero of his and another style icon Billy Bragg. Could have been the double Jack Daniels and coke £6.50 that was clouding the memory. Travelling Band are four albums in now and their gigs get better all the time. Last time I saw them was at the Whiskey Sessions (Victoria Warehouse) with a rockier line up. Last time I saw the Souths was in Koffee Pot whiling some time away. They had no trouble getting served.

Strangely warm and comforting night was made even better at the bar by meeting two of the loveliest gig goers ever. Residents of Rossendale, they had bought tickets the previous Saturday at 3 am after a drunken google of "What's on in Manchester" Real music lovers they were having a great night out. He had just recently taught himself to play banjo (the national instrument of Rossendale) and penned his first tune. An enthused friend had persuaded him to play it at the open mic night at their local. To his initial horror he was suddenly joined on stage by a jamming tin whistle player and a ukulele. To his surprise he then really got into it and said excitedly "It was like being in U2" Now that's the version of U2 I'd have loved to have seen, uke, whistle and banjo. Showing impressive local knowledge or maybe Trip Advisor warned they were well aware of Soup Kitchen's balsa wood walled, indoor septic tank. She braced herself for the experience but still came back dismayed "God, I wish I'd worn my jeans" Ultra friendly people, they even let me ramble on for two long minutes (JD £6.50) about having seen an article calling "Rossendale the new Chorlton" She politely corrected me "Mm I think that's Ramsbottom, it's not far. We are Rossendale... It's the new Kitzbuhel"

Top Tunes; "One year at Sea" South Island Son "Only Waiting"
The Travelling Band

Trove: Levenshulme

You can't be too hard on Levvy as it borders Stockport and there is always some seepage. Turning onto Stockport Boulevard (A6) was treated to a slow paced, middle aged chase between woolly hat on wobbling mountain bike, pursued by angry woolly hat toiling just behind. The only non 4 letter word used was phone. It even crossed at the lights and headed back toward Manchester passed a totally disinterested PCSO.

Levenshulme is one of those places where people always seem to have just bought a new mop head and are sat on a bench having a bottle of beer to recuperate. In this case it was Bavaria Lager 4 for £2, described on ratebeer.com as "OK in Amsterdam but bottled in the UK tastes complete shite"

Although the area as yet is not really known as a hipster haunt, Trove has an almost pure concentration of them, and some form of osmosis draws them through that modestly marked door. I was decidedly the least trendy person to make it in today. Panicked by that hipster vibe I didn't notice all the room at the back of the cafe and ended up basically sitting in the porch. The staff must have thought 'Why is he sat on the windowsill?'

Anyway, that gave me a good view of an old boy sat across the road outside the antique place. Four full bags of shopping at his feet, he shook hands with almost everyone who passed by. His can of choice was steely blue perhaps a vintage Tennent's. Not a care in the world after a few slurps he pulled out some top of the range Bang Olufsen headphones and sat their quite contented. Levvy Cafe culture.

Didn't recognise much on the Trove menu so plumped for the sausage and egg on toast or as they put it Mergues Sausage, fried egg, labneh, carrot, kohlrabi, preserved lemon dressing and sour dough toast. Bewildering but very tasty. Mergues sausages (Algerian recipe) are North African and made of mutton, paprika, fennel, harissa, cumin and coriander.

Not that long ago Levenshulme declared itself an Irish independent state and you can guarantee Guinness of the finest order. A swift early afternoon one in Fiddler's Green was a must. An old Irish fella was just answering his phone as I went in "What? What is it? What are you mithering about now?" This could be the perfect way to discourage a nuisance call but maybe not when it's the wife asking when you'll be back with the shopping. Don't think she was asking if he'd remembered the kohlrabi.

Call finished the barman shouted, "Trevor you having this pint or what?" The stress, he had already ordered another pint. Should he stay or should he go. He left. Nouveau Irish.

Manc Albums (e)

(21) Legendary punk "Another music in a different kitchen" 1978
(22) Salford spin off "It's great when you're straight" 1995
(23) Punk/Funk Factory cassette "The graveyard and the ballroom" 1979
(24) Altrincham dance "Gorgeous" 1993
(25) Oldham's finest "The beast inside" 1991

Madness of Brexit

What could explain Brexit apart from a country that historically has moments of appalling bad taste
1977 Sale of the Century 20.6m devotees
1980 To the Manor Born 21.5m
1988 Bread 20.9m
1993 Big Break 17.5m
2001 Ground Force 12.2 m
2016 Brexit 17.4m
Either that or mad cow disease

Japanese underneath the arches; Umezushi

With a track record that includes walking into Boots the Chemist's goods lift while looking for the food hall in the Arndale wasn't over confident I would be able to find this Japanese restaurant listed as "off the beaten track" The news of road closures only heightened the doubt.

If only Id got the run up right. I started at Shudehill rather than Hanging Ditch which I found later is virtually on the doorstep. On my phone it was quoting the mythical Greengate which seemingly only exists on a town planner's drawing board. More people have found Atlantis than Greengate. Within the space of a few minutes I had asked the help of a Ukrainian, a car salesman, a scouser, a student, a Japanese soldier and a Deliveroo rider. Ukrainian was so happy to be mistaken for a local and that he looked to someone else like he knew where he was going. He gave me a playful backhanded tap on the chest, pulled himself up to his full height and said passionately "Me I am Ukrainian" His ring tone would definitely be the national anthem. No help there. In the Green Quarter (What is that? What colour are the other quarters?) not even the compass in my shoe or phone GPS seemed to be working. At the road crossing, the car salesman's shiny suit was blinding the traffic. This guy was convincing "There is a Japanese restaurant, it's about 15 minutes' walk up there" Can't be there are no arches up Cheetham Hill Rd. Scouser was not as pleased to be thought of as local. On the other side of the road, surely help at last. A student girl pressed about 6 buttons on my phone then confidently marched me back to The Pilcrow where I'd started.

Finally realised which road was Lower Millgate and we were off, passed Vicky station, the Stoller, the Arena steps, under a bridge and straight into a 'Road Closed' sign. Back onto the ring road, left at the light shop. A Japanese soldier emerged from the undergrowth "Is the war over yet?" "No. Is there a Japanese restaurant round here?" "Yeah its about 15 minutes' walk back that way" "Not that one"

By now it was approaching the end of the lunch sitting at 3pm. Finally, a Deliveroo rider assured me "There are two restaurants just down there" Deliverance. You have to bell to get in and the place is unusual in that it looks like a posh builder's office reception. The kind of place you might hire a concrete mixer. The girl on the door was also waitress and shift manager and was exceedingly posh. I couldn't understand any of the menu and she couldn't understand my accent. It didn't help when I got my acronyms mixed up "Even CRS couldn't find this place" I sought her help with the menu "I really don't know. Do I have say one of them with three of them?" "I don't know, how many do you want?" Deadlock. Another chopstick only gaffe but when she saw me struggling like a dolphin trying to read a newspaper she brought over a fork. No ordinary fork, it was like an oversized one you'd give a child in the nursery.

She did explain to me later that they were going to simplify the menu in the future (oik friendly) Cheery heavily tattooed chef (more Newton Heath Reds than Yakuza) shouted "Come back sometime for the night sitting you will enjoy that" Before long I was back at Hanging Ditch. Easy when you know how.

Fantastic Sushi. That octopus was ace. Top pork stew and sticky rice with a bottle of Posh Pop cloudy lemonade and a cheap concrete mixer. 5/5

Looked at my phone and found a message from my friend Ruth "What are you doing walking aimlessly round the ring road. Couldn't stop. Traffic" "Food" She missed a treat. Often think about the old Japanese soldier coming out of the undergrowth in ten years' time "Is Greengate finished yet" "Nope "and troops forlornly back into the bushes again.

Shock news: Umezushi announced it would close for good on October 20th, 2019.Let's hope they are just moving to an idiot proof post code.

Uppermill

What a beautiful relaxing place for a walk or a couple of chilled beers on the banks of The Tame. Oldham has kept this place a well-guarded secret.

Estate agents are often prone to exaggeration hence the "Whalley Range is the new Didsbury" campaign. They could be onto something though with the "Uppermill is the new Chorlton" headlines. In fact, with the beautiful scenery it might just be better.

My morning had started with a fine omelette at 19 Cafe Bar on Lever St. I remember this place when it was far less swish and not so health conscious (Good Food Place) when you could pick up a fine Sausage and black pudding roll. Happily, they have retained their collection of cheesy compilation CDs. Great selection today but a runaway winner. It's Phil Collins's "Easy Lover" that really sets the teeth on edge.

Northern Rail were doing their best to grind Manchester to a halt. If you wanted a day out without a car you were struggling. Greenfield station is just down the road from Uppermill, but the next train was delayed for up to 48 hours.

The only other option was to get the bus from outside Sachas (District 9). Even at 11am on a Bank Holiday morning the lunatic to normal ratio was colossal. An age later the unlimited stop 184 pulled into Oldham town centre (still 25 minutes from our destination) You can marvel at the street names here. My particular favourite is Wellyhole St and it has a place in Oldham history. This was the location of one of the largest prisoner of war camps in the north of England during WW2. Built on the site of a factory it was known as Glen Mill Camp. Just three letters away from someone very famous. Can you imagine if all POW camps had been named after band leaders and humble Oldham had secured the Moonlight Serenader's moniker. What a coup.

With a capacity of 6000 the camp was home to numerous Germans and Italians over the war years. It was the Germans who left the biggest legacy to Oldham though with their love of bad fashion. Problems plagued the Glen Mill camp not least the lack of heating. One prisoner was shot dead during an uprising and was granted a full military funeral in Greenfield cemetery, complete with Nazi salutes and swastika flags.

In an early version of Hunted, there was a mass escape (well seven escapees) The sensible one headed off into deepest Lancashire but was caught. Two were found over the big hill in

Wakefield and four actually made it to Leeds. Whether that was preferable to a prisoner of war camp is questionable. If German television ever did a version of Colditz they could call it Wellyhole St.

An early beery lunch in the Old Library Garden. The bar staff were so jealous 'That's the way to spend a Bank Holiday'. I had a good mooch about marvelling at the posh pooches on show. Some of these dogs were really showboating. Ended up in Bed's beer garden and it was like going to a disfunctional family barbecue. An old shed, rickety garden furniture, bad music and what seemed to be a spat with the neighbours, Betty's Chip Shop. The argument seemed to be over where each establishments patio actually ended. The 'chef' next door objected to where one Bed couple were sat and thankfully, they moved just in time before he launched a huge vat of water out the kitchen door.

All the time Radio Rock Oldham banged out Van Halen, Pat Benatar and Rainbow's "Since you've been gone" Don't think there was any Lever St irony here, this was the current top ten. Top Tunes: "Strange Town" The Jam "Call your name" Karen Elson

Chadderton girl, Karen once wandered into Boss Model Agency on Turner St looking for work and ended up a top model in LA. Other famous Oldhamites: Eric Sykes, Christopher Biggins, Bobby Ball, Mark Owen, Rita and Deirdre.

Wargirl

Back in the YES basement to see Wargirl play one of the gigs of the year. Most impressively it was to a crowd of no more than 30. I watched as the band stood at the back of the room looking dismayed at the sparse attendance. They then went on stage and played a stunning set. Great motivation.

Hailing from the working class, ethnically diverse, creative hub of Long Beach, CA this was brilliant infectious rootsy psyche funk. The best psyche funk band out of Long Beach since War stormed the charts with 'Low Rider' in the 1970's. The neo-political brainchild of musician and producer Matt Wignall, the line-up always consists of three men and three women. Matt's

193

influences of The Clash, Iggy Pop and Santana are stamped all over the sound.

Before the gig I chatted to an old boy sat on a stool near the sound desk. He was a reviewer (Scarletlight.co.uk) and wanted to chat all things music especially the last gig he'd saw, Steve Hackett. I pleaded ignorance on that one. He nodded when I mentioned some of the bands I'd been to see. He recommended Nita Strauss and the strangely familiar sounding Lua Dipa. There was one on the tip of his tongue "You would really enjoy err will get back to you" A look through his notebook and then triumphantly "Got it. Thunderpussy" How do you forget a name like that? Great fella he adored his music.

He told me he had been in a band also called Scarlet Light many moons ago. "We were so close to making it. We had a tour of Germany booked but two of the lads had really good jobs and didn't want to give them up" "Oh no that's terrible. What did they do?" "Well one of them worked for Burtons and the other had a job in Kwiksave"

Saw him taking plenty of notes later. Think he rated the gig as highly as me. 5/5 High class. This band will be huge.

Top Tunes: "People" "Arbolita" "Start a fire" Wargirl

Samantha Parks of Wargirl

Waxahatchee

What could possibly go wrong? A band consisting of siblings with a song beginning Maybe. Danish Mark "Waxahatchee? That should be a trendy crowd with a name like that" I told him they had named themselves after a local landmark a bit like calling yourself Simister Island. Brummie Andy, ex Midlands axeman, was less convinced "I don't know, maybe I just don't get it or maybe they're just not very good" Andy should be kinder, the band are also from Birmingham (Alabama) Duncan who works in the music industry "I don't listen to anything that has a female vocalist" There speaketh the Peveril roundtable jury.

Waxahatchee revolve around twin sisters Katie and Allison Crutchfield and are one of the hardest working bands around. Life is one constant tour. Allison and her band play the warm up set and she's pitched her organ somewhere between Vangelis and Jane Wiedlin's 'Rush hour' Nobody has told the drummer that British music venues aren't allowed air con and he ends up in a sorry sweated down state after playing both sets.

Some of Waxahatchee's earlier music was seriously introspective. Worried siblings asked Katie "Are you OK? Your songs are so sad" She can still nail an emotional ballad on the likes of "Fade", but these days things are much more upbeat with a rockier edge, thanks to new producer John Agnello. Putting crowd favourite 'Silver' at song 2 is a great tactical move and has the place rocking.

My mate the barman is working his socks off tonight. Is it a full moon? This crowd seems soaked in Alabama bourbon. Strangely he's dressed in bright yellow MC Hammer cast offs or were they Hare Krishna's. He might have got a late call to do the shift. Had a chat with an American woman who was wincing with pain pulling at the door to the ladies, like it was the one leading to Fort Knox's strong room. She eyed my brandy like Alien looking at Ripley. In the middle of the bar were a couple one-degree west of paralytic, at one stage he poured his pint into hers when she went to the loo. They must have won tickets in a competition and just gone for it big style. Towards the end they performed a now frowned on ancient gig tradition. Full to the gills they decided to push their way to the front.

If hipster looks could kill. On the edge of the bar near the sound desk were 3 Lancastrian builders who definitely had never featured in oil paintings. One left his pint alone long enough to comment "I've seen her looking worse" Katie has a glorious crumpled look tonight. She spends her life on the road. I'm pretty sure Shane McGowan never had three women eyeing him up and saying "I've seen him look worse"

This seems a massive step forward tonight for a band that is still evolving. All the tracks of the new 'Out in the Storm' album get a great ovation. The encore is an absolute treat. 'La loose' and a fragile acoustic version of 'Fade'. Fantastic. If that wasn't good enough, as the lights went up, the sound man played 'Ca plane pour moi' by Belgian musical genius Plastic Bertrand. A rough translation of the opening line "My cat (Splash!) She's drinking my whisky" What would the Peveril's review panel have made of that?

Top Tune "Brass beam" Waxahatchee

Weather Station

An empty tram seems such a joy at the weekend. Could it be most people were enjoying a night in watching Michael McIntyre's Saturday night? But then at Civic on climbed two young women in garlands. One had a bottle of Lucozade, the other a 2 litre! bottle of Gin. No megaphones required here as they launched into a chorus of "I got 5 on it" They were on the way back to Pride for a second time that day. The atmosphere they said had been unreal. Not sure how long the goodwill towards Pride Festival will last. It seems these days most people consider it one almighty pain in the backside and avoid town like the plague. My main concern is that it may encourage other groups to parade like hordes of James Corden fans or Ed Sheeran groupies.

Just one stop after the ladies arrival, on marched an old boy at Crossacres. Cropped hair, pot marked face with a huge ruck sack clamped to his back. He looked like he'd definitely yomped across the Falklands earlier in life. I was sat at the sideways facing seats and he plonked himself down next to me. The size of the rucksack meant he had to sit side on directly facing the singing duo. Judging his apparent surly demeanour and knowing Wythenshawe's attitude to inclusivity, I pretended to sleep and waited for the onslaught.

He was desperate to tell them something, but it was only after another 'Got 5 on it' (Please let it end) that he just couldn't keep quiet anymore. "I'm retired now, well I work in a care home, but I'm a songwriter" All said in a refined voice. I opened my eyes to check. It wasn't Morrissey was it?

He fumbled about in the rucksack and came up with a page of lyrics and handed it to Gin bottle. "Don't give it her" said Lucozade "She can't even read" Read it she did, with the Crossacres Bob Dylan encouraging her and finishing off each line. Brilliantly he had managed to rhyme "Love's edifice" with "Into the abyss" When the two girls insisted he sing it to them, at first he refused with "I'm a writer not a singer" Gin bottle pleaded with him and went to hand the lyrics back "I don't need that I wrote it" He hadn't taken much persuading. An ok if not quite pitch perfect performance. He then went on to tell the girls that Amy Winehouse had once jokingly threatened him with a restraining order as he kept bombarding her with lyrics. I don't think she was joking.

A couple of stops later, a funky Rihanna lookalike mum got on with her two little ones. The six-year-old was fascinated by the garlands and even the pram sized one in a red McEnroe headband couldn't take her eyes of them. Much jovial banter between Gin, Lucozade, Dylan and Rihanna. Plenty of "Go girl" Yet another "5 on it" brought more laughter. What is the significance?

Gin was getting louder and louder now and used the expression "Muff blocked" to much giggling from Rihanna and a perplexed look from the six-year-old, McEnroe and me. I'm pretty sure it's not a drainage term, most probably something old skool mechanics say to youngsters who have taken their cars in for a MOT.

Manic. Rihanna and kids got off at Barlow Moor and Dylan at Cornbrook minus his lyric sheet. A now teary Gin bottle said, "That was amazing...what just happened?" Not half as bemused as the rest of us. Gullivers is a fantastic venue, the much rowdier sister of the Castle Hotel on Oldham St. This place attracts some serious drinkers, unlike The Castle's creed of cradling one pint of ale all night. The music hall upstairs holds about a hundred, is fantastically basic but has great acoustics. Buck Meek the guitarist from Big Thief is the support act tonight, let out on a solo jolly. Great set by Buck. I bumped into the promoter Chris from Hey Manchester and confused him by repeatedly calling Buck, Chuck. What is it with American names? Pregnant mum to dad on porch in Louisiana "What do you want to call the new-born honey?" "Chuck" "We've already got a Chuck ""Buck then" Like The Castle there is no stage access left or right. To get on stage the artists must make their way from the back of the venue through the throng. It was easy for Buck with his "I'm a musician hat" on and guitar strapped to his back. Not so for the diminutive Tamara Lindeman of headline band, Weather Station. Faced with the wall to wall backs, she tried four of five times to prise open a route to the stage, like a child trying to fight their way on to a football terrace.

Tamara's songs are brilliant, like novellas set to music.

What an epic skill. This is true songcraft. If only I'd got a copy of Dylan's lyric sheet. I could have handed it to Tamara and had a worldwide smash. At one time Tamara apologised for herself and the band (apart from the Belgian drummer) being from uncool Ontario. It's a shame we didn't get the chance to apologise for Oldham St.

At the end she asked what she should play for an encore and almost everyone shouted 'Transmission' There is history here. Looking bashful Tamara turned to the band "Err I don't think we even know what key that song is in" Again there was plenty who could advise her. It was only on getting home and checking on YouTube I realised they really don't know what key it is in. After two encores bassist and Belgium drummer had fought their way to the merch stall at the back only to see Tamara beckoning them back for a third. Back they went again "Scuse me, scuse me" Exhausting stuff. At the real end I asked the bassist which CD to buy. He said without hesitation "Definitely that one" "Why what's up with the other one?" He'd had enough now and introduced Tamara.

Top Tunes: "Thirty" Weather Station "Into the abyss" Crossacres
Bob
Most annoying "I got 5 on it" Luniz YouTube moment
"Transmission" Weather Station

Where were you when....?

England won the world cup. I was at Warhorse at The Lowry
Theatre. What an absolute blinder. What skills in bringing them
puppet horses to life. Visually stunning, technically brilliant and
makes you blub like a baby.

Across the square in a more surreal world, the bars were thronged
with people watching England drub footballing giants Panama 6-
1. The next day highbrow radio sports pundit Jason Cundy
trumpeted "We can win the thing now, and Spurs can expect
£600m bids for Harry Kane in the summer" Surprisingly neither
happened.

Our worst moment in the theatre came in added time. The whole
place was trying a collective "Hold it together. Hold it together"
As the lights came up a young girl on the row in front bellowed at
her mam "Why are you crying?" For a second everyone thought
she was talking to them. Mind you her mum's glasses had been
on top of her head and down again more often than an Eric
Morecambe sketch. A dead give-away. I hung around at the end,
my hay fever had been terrible throughout or maybe just
overjoyed at Harry's hat trick.

Think I got away with it. Spectacular show 5/5.

Gusto

Have you ever been heading for some pub grub and then been
captivated by one of them restaurant deal blackboards? Couldn't
resist a visit to Gusto (Deansgate) after it enticed me in when I
was all set for the Lost Dene.

I must have looked like I'd been dragged through the privets, (the
favoured Lost Dene look) as I was initially greeted like Ian
Paisley at the doors of The Vatican. All that was needed to
complete the look was a battered old brown suitcase and they

would have been convinced I'd just checked out of Holiday Inn, Strangeways.

Great buzzing atmosphere for a Monday afternoon. All the posh people were seated to the right (no surprises there) while us plebs occupied the left which was great for me as I was right near the excellent Manchester Legends mural.

When Gusto opened in this Grade 2 listed building on the corner of Lloyd St in 2014, they commissioned artist Michael J Browne (Moss Side and Rome) to paint a Renaissance style mural of Manchester icons. What a varied collection he came up with Joule, Gaskell, Delaney, Turing, Rutherford, Bacon, Pankhurst, Dalton, Duffy, Kirsty, Gibb R, and Gallagher N.

The centrepiece of the mural is Central Library which once temporarily occupied this space. The theme shows angels carrying books of knowledge from the past into the future. Will they be charged for the late returns? It left me wondering who will be most fondly remembered in 100 years' time. The Bee Gees or Oasis. Robin Gibb once said surprisingly "I sing with my heart not my voice" If you've ever heard High Flying Birds you know that's definitely anatomically different from Noel.

The prawns, tagliatelle, gnocchi, roast chicken, spuds, Rioja and tap water were all lovely. I always think you look more authentic if you eat peasant type food with your fingers, but from the looks I was getting maybe this doesn't stretch to the roast potatoes. Elegant décor, smiley staff, gorgeous food and I even got into the Caro Emerald soundtrack.

Turned left for my regular trip down to Atlas Bar for a couple of large 'Gin of the week'. I was much taken by both the Daffy's Gin and the Goddess bottle. As my first finished off the bottle the knowledgeable and ever cheerful barman said, "Do you want the empty?" "Of course," Then thought that's not going to look too good climbing on the tram with an empty bottle of gin. So, another member of staff got me a plain brown paper bag from the kitchen. The kind they used in the prohibition. Sorted, image is everything.

Top Tune "The Ghost of You "Caro Emerald "A Night Like This" Caro Emerald

Withington

Of the four neighbouring districts of Withington, Didsbury, Fallowfield, and Burnage, you can always spot a Withingtonian. Something unique about their appearance and character.

As children our dad used to regale us with his tales of Withington and the charms of the White Lion. Our ears would only prick up though when he mentioned the old horse trough and tap that stood opposite the pub. I'm a firm believer that the distinct character of the locals comes from generations supping from that little white enamel cup that was chained to the trough. The trough was inscribed "That ye may drink, both ye and your cattle and your beasts"

It once disappeared and showed up mysteriously in a farmer's field in Heald Green. That was some drunken prank. The trough was returned to Copson St and the farmer got a new tin bath as a replacement.

Largely rural until the mid-19th century, Withington didn't officially become part of Manchester until 1904. Its first recorded mention came in 1186 as a farmstead in a willow copse. Over the years it passed between most of the famous local landowning families, Hathersage, Longford, Moseley and the Egertons. Wilmslow Rd was a turnpike road that headed south from the city to the sticks. Horse trams travelled this route until 1902.

Fares ranged from the luxury of inside 6d to the misery of outside in the drizzle 4d. The electrification of the line after that brought a brand-new sparkling station called Withington and West Didsbury. In 1915 the locals were described as "wealthy with a rather pronounced air of culture" On a recent visit here with my sister H we popped into Fuel cafe, hankering after a steak butty, forgetting the local new age leanings. H ended up with double decker Haloumi (the cheese that doesn't taste of cheese) and I had a Falafel (which Google says is a burger made from chickpea and fava beans) A really cultured bunch and lunch. I once tried to go to a gig here but barred myself as it was just too trendy. This afternoon was enlightened by an old West Indian guy going from table to table saying "Life is a gift not a curse. Remember" He went to every table but ours, the one distinct advantage of having a residual Wythenshawe frown. When he left, I asked a bearded one at the counter "How often does he come in?" Huge sigh of relief "Not as often as he used to"

Legend has it that when the local church of St Pauls got a new organ in the 1840s, Mendelssohn just happened to be in town on a city break. The vicar managed to get Felix to play a few tunes on the new keyboard.

Ernest Rutherford the father of nuclear physics lived on Wilmslow Rd in the early 20th century. John Mahoney, Frazier's dad in the TV series was brought locally. Hough End playing fields used to be known as Alexandra Park Aerodrome. In 1910 Frenchman, Louis Paulhan won the Daily Mail cup for the first flight from London to Withington. Paulhan Rd near Fog Lane Park is named after the legendary French aviator.

The Red Lion is a listed building dating from the 17th century when people were a lot smaller hence the dangerously low lintels. The landlord for many years was the tached Crown Green bowling genius Noel Burrows. The Red had its periods of great popularity and hugely contrasted with its curious less friendly now defunct neighbour, The Turnpike. When you opened the door to the Turnpike you got a full re-enactment of the scene from American Werewolf, every head in the pub turns and glared at you.

The White Lion dated from 1841 but is now a Sainsbury's Local. If you look closely though some of the old features can still be seen in the shop. The recesses of the fireplace and even some stained-glass windows. It even has a well out in the backyard. Next door to the White was the old cinema, The Scala, which was more correctly known as The Flea Pit. Further down the road are the green tiles of The Albert, bought as part of a three-house deal by Thomas Holt in 1852. One kept as a residence, one became a shop and the third was the boozer. It was first mentioned as a pub in 1897. If an American asked to see a traditional spit and sawdust pub, you could take them here, even though for a time The Albert didn't have a floor, never mind sawdust.

The Waterloo pub was demolished in 1993 but has a better back story than Sea Biscuit. Local man Bill Foulkes found an emaciated greyhound wandering the city streets. Bill called the hound Brigadier and nursed him back to health. To pay Bill back,

Brigadier went on to win the prestigious hare coursing title The Waterloo Cup in 1866. Bill bought a local hotel with his winnings and named it The Waterloo. On the pub's demolition, houses were built on the site and it was named Brigadier Close. Indeed, he was, the old greyhound had been buried in the grounds under a plaque "In memory of a faithful friend" His image is captured in a painting by Henry Calvert called 'Brigadier'
Unexpected Plaque: 42 Everett Rd the birthplace of Hollywood legend Robert Donat

Wythenshawe and the two Johns

The construction of the Garden City started in the 1920's on a vast area of the ancient rural settlements of Northern Etchells, Baguley and Northenden. It was the last area to be incorporated into the city of Manchester in 1931. The original plan was to give each residence the choice of what to have at the front of the house, either an Oak tree or a Silver Birch. A larger choice is available today, either a car on bricks, some pub garden furniture or a trampoline. David Cameron once made a video here and a plethora of celebs and luminaries have been born here or made it their home.

Country and Western sensation and sometime pugilist Tyson Fury can often be seen twirling his championship belts above his head outside B&M's after checking his balance at the TSB. Top of the Pops regulars Johnny Marr and Jason Orange are locals. Method acting devotee Simon Gregson (Steve McDonald) was born here and renowned thespian Harry H Corbett (Harold from Steptoe) was a former resident.

Attracted by that Cheshire border air, even world leaders have made Wythenshawe their home. Diminutive Irish president Michael D Higgins spent a post grad year here but was never spotted due to the height of the privets. One of the world's most famous people in 2019 Samwell Tarly from Game of Thrones (real name John Bradley West) was a former pupil of St Paul's. The Metro system has brought hope and outsiders into the area. Japanese tourists excitedly checking the map "Are we in Manchester yet?" before realising that it takes 13 stops to get out of Wythenshawe. Outside the packs of wild beasts roaming around are actually on their way to Civic. A young hawk often sits on the fence of Sale Golf Club across the motorway from Northern Moor station, staring anxiously over to see if any gangs of feral pigeons are heading its way.

One tram driver totally stumped at how to finish his message that the tram would terminate here due to yet another car on the tracks announced the terrifying "Final Destination, Northern Moor" What a film that would be. Born and bred Marcus Rashford wears enough bling on an average night out to buy the whole estate.

A characteristic Wythenshawe people share with our scouse cousins is to announce where they are from to completely uninterested or horrified strangers when first meeting them. For me this extends to waitresses. Knowing the owner of One88 restaurant in Whitefield was famous Wythenshawe chef, David Gale,I announced, "I'm from Wythenshawe as well" and she gave me a look usually reserved for people seeing Michael Gove out jogging for the first time. Part horror part sympathy. I may as well have said "Hi, I've got all over body hives"

Along with Wythenshawe Airport and hospital, many large employers have striven to keep the locals off the street. Shell, Duerr's (jam) and Timpson's (cobblers) have given employment to thousands. I spent two long spells at Ferranti and my favourite character was a huge ex Welsh Guardsman, John Evans. Proud of his Valleys upbringing and native tongue, John would greet everyone with a cheery 'Bore da' He was keen to teach us some other Welsh phrases. He taught me one greeting but strangely only used it when senior management were around. He would rush up with a big smile on his face and say his bit and I would reply with what he had painstakingly taught me. Years later when trying to translate the words I realised that even though he might well have been saying "Hello and how are you today?" I was definitely replying with something stronger than "Fine thanks, now you go off and have a good day yourself"

Just down the road from Ferranti, little now remains of the brilliant brutalist buildings of Shell. The employees were lucky to have a classy social club where much team building was done. That was until the 1990's when a new breed of middle managers spawned by Margaret Thatcher arrived. To the staff's horror, everyone at Shell was to be re-appraised. First in was local hero GF. The others sat waiting in trepidation like Apprentice candidates on interviews day. After some time, GF returned "How did it go?" GF relieved "I think it went well, he started talking French to me" "Why what did he say?" "You seem to have a very laissez-faire attitude to work"

A more venerable John Evans amiably runs Shell Racing Club to this day. The first race is always the most important. That's the one from the turnstiles to get the best table in the bar. Last year at Uttoxeter we mistimed the last-minute charge from pub to course and bumped into the horses being led from stable to paddock. "What do you call one of them?" It's not the done thing once ensconced and clutching a Guinness to ever emerge from the bar. In days of yore we wouldn't have had to travel as far as Staffordshire for our fix as Manchester traditionally had its own racecourse. Every year on Whit Sunday a naked 5-furlong sprint for colts would take place at the track on Kersal Moor, Salford. (the relay had been banned by H&S) In 1769 one of the contestants was Roger Aytoun, a strapping 6' 4" Scotsman who on his clothed days strutted the streets of Manchester in full military uniform, even though as yet he had not been in the Forces (see Mark Francois)

An interested spectator that day was Barbara Minshull, a rich widow whose family owned much of the land around Piccadilly, Whitworth and Portland St. Much taken by Roger's running style she proposed that day and within 3 weeks Babs (aged 65) and the Scottish streaker (25) were married. Scandalous.

Gregarious Rog liked a pint and was so relaxed on the wedding day, he had to be propped up throughout by a mate who was probably whispering "Remember Hough Hall" to him. The Moston residence was to be Bab's wedding gift to her husband. Roger's cunning plan slightly backfired as beguiled Barbara lived for another 14 years.

Whiling the time away before his inheritance, the old rogue set about recruiting his own Manchester Volunteers Regiment, the 72nd Regiment of Foot. There is some dispute as to where he got his nickname, Spanking Roger. Babs insisted it was down to his fondness for a brawl. His regiment recruiting policy involved walking into the roughest pubs and starting a fight. He would pick his 'volunteers' from whoever remained after the skirmish. Amazingly the regiment successfully defended the Rock of Gibraltar for many years from Spanish and French incursions. The siege was chronicled by a soldier called John Drinkwater, obviously not a friend of Johns with a name like that. In the whole 5 years Roger's name was never mentioned, probably back home in the attic at Hough Hall.

Roger 'returned' to Manchester in triumph when the siege ended in 1783 and though probably not much of a sprinter now, the old cad went on to marry another rich widow in his native Scotland. His and Barbara's legend are engraved in Manchester history. Together forever, Aytoun St and Minshull St sit alongside each other in Piccadilly.

Once is usually enough for anyone

Y'alright Luv

If unprepared local expressions can take you completely by surprise. "I've been asked if I'm alright so many times since I've been in Manchester, I'm beginning to think I'm not" Anna Burch To add to Anna's paranoia, she had only recently shaved off her dark tresses for the full-on Sinead O'Connor look. Was it a success she wondered at the end? Did people think she was self-haircutting? From afar it looked drastic, up close mega cool.

Despite Mali Hayes's waistline worries weighing heavy on my mind couldn't resist another visit to Pieminster before Gullivers. Mexicow with mash and a Punk IPA. Great sustenance. Do other people get lost in the NQ? For me Pieminster's door is part of a Bermuda Triangle, along with Terrace Bar and Matt and Phreds. Do their doors change location each time? And that's before a can of Punk.

I'd forgotten the printed ticket so like a very young or very old person had written out my name and the booking reference on a piece of paper. When I handed it to the lad on the desk like a school note the look on his face said "I am an earthling you know. Why didn't you just say your name? Two bearded American lads hanging around after sharing a 'herbal cig' outside looked on quizzically, like they were watching a card trick. He stamped my hand and as I walked off, he shouted me back "And there's your ticket for work tomorrow" Along with my school note I had also handed him a horse racing tip for the following day, also written down in careful capital letters. The horses name was Swerved. Much chuckling from the young Americans.

Not a full house yet for the lovely support act Finola but it did include three other Americans. The girls in front of me were students and must have been studying moderation. So well behaved they had just one drink each to my three bottles of Erdinger. From what they said they had already encountered the two frat pack lads. The bearded ones had told them that they had gone to the same High School as Anna. A high risk chat up line especially as Anna then walked in to watch part of Finola's gig. Would only have taken a "Did them guys go to your school?" Anna's gig was great and got a rousing reception. She even toasted the crowd with a whisky or two and handed out a couple

of glasses of hard liquor to her most ardent followers. She is yet another huge Morrissey fan! Did all of America grow up listening to him and Mark E Smith? What a collaboration that would have been though not sure it could ever have happened after 1984's Fall song CREEP was rumoured to be about the Trafford legend "He reads books: of the list book club". Anna had a very individual interpretation of Smith's songs as she revealed she had always misheard the lyrics. Great craic at the merch table. Finola's dad was doing her sales and Anna had revealed that tomorrow's gig was in Leeds. I was just launching into a "Bloody hell Leeds!" when Finola said "My dad's from Leeds. Careful" Up lumbered an old boy to see Anna "Now about mishearing Morrissey lyrics..." and he was off. Think he had written down a little list. Time for a whisky. Tip for the top 2020.
Top Tune: "Tea soaked Letter "Anna Burch "Keep a Vow "Finola
The merch stand can be a very odd place. One innovative idea we really don't need to catch on was offered by Marika Hackman at the end of her gig at Band on the Wall. "If you come up to the merch stall afterwards you've got the chance to win our sweaty stage gear" They re-appeared in forensic type onesies with work clobber in hand. This really isn't an offer you would want to hear from Black Grape.

YES

The old auction house next to the Lass o Gowrie is now a sparkling new music venue. It's interesting that if you were buying tickets for gigs right up to the opening night it seemed to have a range of different names. Did the boss ring marketing the night before "Look have you got a name yet for this place?" "Err yes" Really hope instead it's named after the 1970's chintz rockers, Yes. Jon Anderson and Rick Wakeman's band were hugely important to the history of music. Their 1973 album Topographic Oceans was so bad that things had to change. The organ and warbling concept double album had only 4 tracks. Four very very long tracks. Punk rock was born not long after.
All four floors are very different. The ground floor bar and pizza kitchen has a great atmosphere. Maybe the pizza menu hints at

who they are trying to attract. No meat bonanza here. The best seller in the opening week was the Aubergine Genie. The 'gine Genie features marinated aubergine, paesana olive, peanuts, chermoula and vegan mozzarella. Other pizza toppings include fried sage pistou and sumac labneh. You could have your five for the day here. Five things you've never heard of.

On the terrace bar I really did fancy demolishing a Bloody Southerner but couldn't resist, the kegged in house, Bourbon Old Fashioned. Happiness in a glass. This bar is pretty spectacular and what a bonus for the roll your own brigade. An actually pleasant smoking area that won't make them feel like a banished tribe. Really great vibe hope it stands the test of time.

The basement has been left gloriously sparse and looks a great stage to play. Tonight, at the Songs for Walter gig the excitement of a new venue seems to have got to many. The chattering was so loud you couldn't even hear the support act introduce himself. Never did find out who he was.

Shaking my head in dismay the lad next to me at the bar seemed to share the pain. He later asked, "You must have been in a band?" "No" "My band is called The Buffalo Riot, I'm the drummer, we have nothing like this place at all in Liverpool. It's great"

He told me he was great friends with Laurie Hulme (Songs for Walter) which I doubted till Laurie spotted him from the stage and gave him a namecheck and thumbs up. SFW have a truly dedicated following mostly it does seem of fellow musicians. A genuine endorsement. Laurie refreshingly says "I've never wanted to write about love. I like writing about peculiarities in people, the bizarre world we live in and the strange things we do" Laurie has a song about the long forgotten Peterloo II. "The battle of Bexley Square" In the depression of 1931, 10 000 men and women marched from town to Salford to protest against the oppression of the working class. They wanted free coal for the unemployed, free milk for the under 5s and a rejection of the proposed 10% cut in unemployment benefits. At the time the unemployment rate in Salford was about 33%.

When the protest reached Bexley Sq., they were ambushed by baton wielding thugs. The mounted police. One of those present in the crowd was Walter Greenwood who would immortalise the story in his book "Love on the Dole"

Not a favourite of Esther McVey.

Top Tunes: "Meet me at The Empire" Songs for Walter "1996"

The Buffalo Riot

I saw Jess Williamson playing the first floor Pink Room in the early weeks of YES. A bit of a gamble every single thing in here is pink.

Think Lemmy might have found it a struggle. Much has been made of pink's calming effect and it does seem to produce a relaxed and receptive crowd.

The strangest aspect here is the stage door. It really does look like the band are entering through the disabled toilets. The key selling point is the so impressive NASA approved sound system. That space probe playing music as it careers through the outer edges of our universe has the very same system. You can imagine some alien cutting the grass on a Sunday morning and this ramshackle can flies overhead but it's playing crystal clear versions of We are the champions and Goodbye Norma Jean.

Jess looks stunning in the pink and anyone who writes a song about mortality after spotting the first white hairs of aging around her dog's eyes is ok by me. Her nan had a slightly different view of her when she heard Jess had written a song called 'Love on the piano'

Top Tunes: "I see the white" "White bird" Jess Williamson

Jess in the pink

York away

It is wonderful to get the chance to see a favourite band in a city you have never visited. Hurray for the Riff Raff are playing in an ex working men's club in York. Priceless.

I thought I was excited, but it was nowhere near the fervour of the five young tots on the Piccadilly train from Heald Green, on their way to see "Room on the Broom" at the Lowry. Just one female guardian, I hope she had re-enforcements meeting her in town. Only partly through the journey and she already deserved a medal for bravery

Piccadilly station approach and it's too early for my Trans-Pennine so a swift Botanist gin in B-Lounge (forever The Brunswick) Within minutes a lad has been turfed out for being too drunk. The barmaid said calmly "I heard you shouting outside. I think you've had enough" Time 11.20 Before storming briefly into the Premier League, Huddersfield was solely known as the home of Standard Fireworks. The jingle 'Light up the sky with Standard Fireworks' was the catchiest of its generation, long before Shake n vac stuck in the nation's craw.

For the Huddersfield to York connection we all cram into the one unbooked carriage and quickly a hero with a wandering eye emerges. Young Darryl in shiny shoes, shinier trousers and pristine white shirt is on a mission to get the attention of the young student girl who has ended up sat opposite him. Despite his tender years he is recruiting for "BP Oil" on his phone. Too busy to hang up, the call continues as he buys a coffee off the trolley dolly, who was really a huge Asian guy with a Salford accent. Unimpressed "BP Oil? Aah petrol pump" Manchester savagery in Yorkshire. The object of Darryl's affections looked even less impressed.

York looked dazzling in the August heat. The Minster, museum gardens and Ouse looked stunning. Not forgetting that old wall built by the Romans seemingly so they could peer into people's bedrooms.

I was staying at The Cavalier and whilst checking directions walking across town noticed it was next to the YSH. Must be decent it's next to a Youth Hostel. Only when I got there, I saw it stood for Yorkshire Sexual Health. The Cav was great. Relaxed, clean and most importantly very cheap and you could even get English telly. The receptionist recommended the nearby Black Horse for a bite to eat. The bite turned out to be a beef and veg stew inside a huge Yorkshire pudding, washed down with a Timothy Taylor's 'Boltmaker'

Champion.

Apart from Japanese tourists the largest group in town today are Darlington fans who are down for a crunch match with York City. Congregated outside the Kings in traditional North East football garb, vests and slightly flared denims. The crunch ended 0-0. Time to head to the much trendier Nook on Castlegate. A pint of a really lovely local beer The Flummoxed Farmer from Ainsty Ales. Apparently brewed by the barman's uncle in his back garden. Aren't they all? By the time I wandered down Fossgate the Yorkshire pudding had worn off. Ambiente tapas looked a good idea

Turned out to be a great idea. I ordered a pint and checked out the menu. The hugely enthusiastic manager made a beeline. They had just received a delivery of the very best Padron Peppers. There was to be no argument that was my starter. The Estrella Galicia was fine but "What you really need with peppers is..."and he was off. The peppers arrived seared and sprinkled with sea salt and olive oil. My new friend arrived seconds later beaming triumphantly "Oloroso!! with those peppers and this sherry you will believe you are in Galicia" Food hedonism and the sherry was free.

This was International day; the waitress was Italian and asked politely where I was from. "Manchester?" Her jaw dropped open "I thought you were German" Great host with lovely staff. The only thing they couldn't help with was the elasticated trousers I needed on the way out. Just a few yards down the road is the brilliant mega trendy Fossgate Social. Sat happily outback listening to two couples earnestly discussing Polanski. Sadly, I didn't make the planned trip to the much-exalted Inn of Trembling Madness, instead just a swift one pre gig in The Priory. I was expecting a voice to say "We've been expecting you"

A brilliant performance by Alynda and Hurray for the Riff Raff despite it not being a capacity crowd. I discussed this with possibly Hartlepool's trendiest couple. They told me they had once driven all the way to Gullivers, Manchester to see their favourites American Aquarium and there was only 20 people there. Didn't dare tell them I was thinking American who? Must be hard to be a hipster in Hartlepool.

Sensational gig by HFTRR. A decade into her career and after 6 very different albums Alynda Segarra is still very much the tortured creative standing up for oppressed peoples of every ilk. As a Puerto Rican punk run away from The Bronx, she immersed herself in the music and style of wherever the freight train took her. Americana, Country, Blues, Roots, Folk are all here.

These days she rails against Trump and berates her fellow artists for not making their voices and fears heard "Now the poets were dying of a silence disease"

Found a hearty breakfast the next day at Number 84 Micklegate but with a Priory sized hangover didn't quite appreciate the Oasis soundtrack or the fact everything seemed to come with smashed avocado. I asked the waitress "What is it?" "It's a sort of fruit. Will put it in a side dish for you" So glad she did. Superfood? Bet the Darlington fans have never touched it.

Top Tunes "Hungry Ghost" HFTRR "Man I'm supposed to be" American Aquarium

Zlatan in Stockholm

Sweden was everything you would expect and couldn't afford. Hugely over expensive. Two young lads on my flight were quoted £120 by a taxi driver for the short trip from Arlanda airport to Stockholm town centre. Luckily, I was staying close to the airport in Masta and the hotel operated an airport shuttle bus. Per the owner was the shuttle driver, head cook and bottle washer. He was there within five minutes and only charged a fiver. Loose change in Sweden. Broby Gard hotel was a ringer for a 1950s American motel, set in genuine isolation and even had creaky ceiling fans. Anthony Perkins would have loved it.

Next morning, I was shocked to find I was the only guest and there were no other staff. Even so a trusting Per happily disappeared off to walk his Italian greyhounds leaving me manning the front desk. When he returned, he guided me into the dining room and set about preparing a feast. Maybe he wasn't too sure how many guests he had because he made a huge smorgasbord of fresh food. As he laboured, he translated from the radio with great intensity the story of the mining town of Kiruna. It was being moved lock stock and barrel two miles east of its present location as the intensity of the drilling meant it was in danger of falling into a self-made sinkhole. The only problem being the new homes would be vastly more expensive than the present ones. Indignant Per. This was a Swedish scandal. Anyway, by the time he'd finished translating there was not much of the 'bord left. You have to get your money's worth over here. Per looked even more shocked. Still he made more coffee and gave me two apples. "Maybe you could feed Zlatan on your way to the train station" Zlatan was his pet pig who lived in a barn down the road. I asked the swine about Kiruna and ponytails and there was not a flicker of interest, better things to worry about. Per was a good guy and that was one cool pig.

Manc Albums Quiz Answers:

(1) Magazine (2) M People (3) The Fall (4) A Guy Called Gerald (5) Cherry Ghost (6) Elbow (7) Dutch Uncles (8) Starsailor (9) Swing out Sister (10) Slow Readers Club (11) The Ting Tings (12) Northside (13) Money (14) Monaco (15) Everything Everything (16) The Mock Turtles (17) The Whip (18) Marion (19) James (20) I Am Kloot (21) Buzzcocks (22) Black Grape (23) A Certain Ratio (24) 808 State (25) Inspiral Carpets

www.ingramcontent.com/pod-product-compliance
Lightning Source LLC
Chambersburg PA
CBHW061401280526
45784CB00001B/331